G000154629

ACROSS

CHINA

IN 250 PAGES

BY TUDOR FINNERAN

ABOUT
ACROSS CHINA IN 250 PAGES

By travelling across China in 250 pages you will visit the dynasties, explore the cultural hubs, understand the mentalities and engage with the most unique aspects of society... but more importantly you will gain a fantastic understanding of the modern nation through eight core focuses.

Whether China is your home or holiday destination there is one guarantee - it will effect you in the future. China's customs, consumer demands, politics and even dating habits have more of a global impact than most small nations. As the scale and spirit of this once mystical land grows so too does the need to really understand it. Part of the reason for this book is to equip the reader to not just understand the change, but appreciate the nation's very DNA and make the most of it.

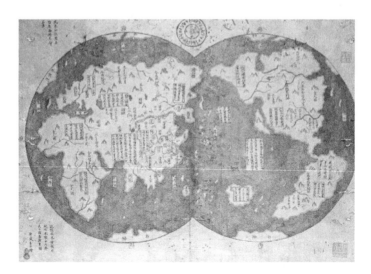

ABOUT THE AUTHOR

Tudor has worked in museums, across the markets, for the Government and in several international organisations. His personal ventures have always focused on China, whether it be the app - Chopstick Champion which he developed at age 19, to his advisory capacity on startups, to his work in public policy. His current projects are all geared toward China and over the next few years he will travel the nation on foot to produce a cutting edge docuseries. When not working you can find him up a mountain or volunteering at his local Church.

PAST PROJECTS

Other works by this author include "Across Africa in 250 Pages, An Unofficial Investigation into the Nazis and National Socialist Era, An Unofficial Investigation into the Soviet Union and Exploring the British Empire.

CURRENT

Current creative works include a screenplay and fiction book set in the Golden Age of Dynastic China, which is soon to be released. and a volume on wealth management, titled 'Making Coin, An interesting guide to making money, wealth management, investing, banking, property and startups' which explores modern entrepreneurship through the lens of environmental and societal opportunities.

Outside of writing, advising and preparing for the next venture Tudor is establishing a working startup model for urban development, which utilizes high profit but sustainable infrastructure and businesses.

LETTER FROM THE AUTHOR

First and foremost, thank you for your interest and purchase.
I wrote this saga on all things China to take you on a journey across the nation and it's history. As China becomes more important (to all of our lives) it is of growing importance to be familiar and knowledgeable of China's history, thought, politics, industry, society, differences, culture and change.

Aside from being fascinating it is also valuable. The content within will equip you with everything you need to know about China, whether you are living, doing business or holidaying there. As the misconceptions and misunderstandings also grow an unbiased guide through the subjects mentioned above is essential, but more importantly they add to your experience and interaction with the modern nation.

CONTENTS

8 CHAPTERS – 8 FOCUSES

CHAPTER I - HISTORY

CHAPTER II - CHINESE THOUGHT

CHAPTER III – CHINESE POLITICS

CHAPTER IIII – CHINESE INDUSTRY

CHAPTER V – CHINESE SOCIETY

CHAPTER VI - DIFFERENCES
As a Foreigner in China
(You must Understand)

CHAPTER VII - CULTURE

CHAPTER VIII – THE CHANGE IN CHINA

Dedicated to

My Grandparents,
WENDY AND KEITH

Enjoy and 恭喜發財

Prologue

"I did not tell half of what I saw, for I knew I would not be believed."

The words of the great explorer Marco Polo are as true today as they were 12th century.

CHINESE HISTORY

1

"Our greatest glory is not in never falling, but in rising every time we fall."
- Confucius

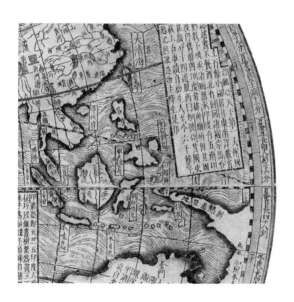

PREHISTORY OF CHINA

The pre-history of North and South China are very different, the history of it's East and West even more so. China has been labelled the cradle of civilisation and as time progresses and archaeological finds increase this is becoming more and more true.

Recent archaeological discoveries reveal more evidence which indicate that ancient China is where mankind became civilised. The remains being found in China are drastically different to Australasia and Africa. The excavations reveal the use of tools, fire, buildings and development in an era when the rest of early man was still cave dwelling.

The early humanoid remains being found in China are for the most part being identified as either homo sapien or homo erectus. Excavations outside of China which date to a similar time period are often more closely related to the ape man, an earlier form of humanoid. This indicate that these early settlers had evolved or bred with other species of early man since leaving the South East Europe or the African continent.

Of all the recent discoveries there have been three major breakthroughs. They further support the theory as China being the first home or provenance of civilised man.

The first of these discoveries was the 'Yuanmou Man.' He was found in Yunnan Province in South-West China. He lived approximately 1.7 million years ago and resembled a monkeys form with the features of a human.

The next major breakthrough was the discovery of the 'Lantian Man.' The Lantian was dated at 1.15 million years old and from the early Paleolithic Age. His appearance was very different to the 'Yuanmou man.' He had a greater cranial capacity and much less hair. This discovery was proof of early age non ape-human life in China.

The final of the big three discoveries was the famous 'Peking Man.' Discovered in Northern China's Shaanxi Province, he was related to the 'Lantian Man.' They were related by virtue of being in the same category of Homo Erectus, except the Peking man was at a more developed state. He is dated to have lived just 500,000 years ago. The mystery of the missing Peking man is equally as fascinating, as the remains went missing during World War II.

THE GENETICS OF THE NATION

From these early humans came a civilised era of early communal dwelling humans. From this point the foundations of Ancient China were set in motion.

Discoveries show that the early 'people' of China shared a common genetic line with Eurasian and Caucasian people. Recent genetic research further supports via the Neanderthal gene being found more commonly in East Asians, North Asians, Eurasians and European Caucasians.

Next to no Neanderthal genes have been found in African genetic lines. In fact the genetic lines of East African's (notably Somali and Ethipian people) have a different genetic ancestor all together, named the Herto Man.

This leads us to believe the early tribes of migrating people who travelled across the European to Asian landmass interbred. Thus they evolved differently with traits of the Neanderthal. This increased the genetic and physical proximity from the traits of the older human species in Africa.

From this moment those who would settle in Europe travelled West, over the mountain ranges and would face a land locked ice age later on.

Those who settled in now modern China crossed the Asian landmass, frozen Siberian tundra, South Asian jungles, mountains and the Gobi Desert. This occurred over many thousands of years and influenced the evolution and features of those ancient people even further.

As these early people crossed both desert and ice shelves the epicanthic fold in the eyelid evolved to reduce the intense glare. The physical digestive system also developed to become more arduous and able to live off a Nomadic diet, but less tolerant of milk, wheat and alcohol.

This journey was calorie intensive, with intense food scarcity leading to malnutrition. Many leading anthropologists attribute this to the shorter stature of East Asians, which in turn allowed for greater energy efficiency. As living conditions and a food surplus increase in modern China the overall height and built of the nation is beginning to change once again.

Once the migrations was completed, those who settled in modern China had access to fertile soils, rich lakes full of fish, mountain terrains for hunting and a comfortable climate.

Over several thousand years these early settlers would become the first in human civilisation to build permanent structures from carved rock and compressed bricks made of mud. It was from this moment that the ancient history of China really began.

ANCIENT CHINA

To this day China has over 3,500 years of written history. This is the longest continuous history and known timeline of any country in the world. A chronological order of China's history began in 7000BC and ended in 1912AD.

It starting with;

The Peiligang Culture, 裴李岗文化,
7000 to 5000 BC

The Peiligang culture lined the central banks of the Yellow River in what is now Henan Province. These early people of central China are documented as the oldest Neolithic culture. They practised agriculture and even raised livestock, unlike many other societies at this time who still lived as nomadic hunter-gatherers.

Remnants of advanced hunting tools have been found dating to this time, but more impressively the Peiligang people are believed to have fished and farmed the carp species.

In addition to this advanced knowledge of seeds, and an unparalleled ability to adapt their fields for dry seasons or floods, they had both residential and separate burial areas; Something not practised by other cultures for another 4000 years.

Their settlement has also revealed an advanced knowledge of building structures via compression methods, as well as being the first culture in the world to have made pottery.

The Cishan Culture 磁山文化
5400 to 5100 BC

Whether the Cishan culture carried on, traded with or even visited Peiligang settlements remains a mystery. What is known is the Cishan culture built on and progressed Peiligang knowledge and skills.

The Cishan culture is thought to have begun 400 years after the fall of the Peiligang, but contains many similar components and traits. They too had developed an advanced knowledge of farming and even employed tools like the sickle, knives and shovels to farm millet.

Hand made pottery has also been found within their settlement, located in the North of China, now Hebei Province.

The Yangshao Culture 仰韶文化
5000 to 3000 BC

The Yangshao culture refers to a Neolithic community found along the middle stretch of the Yellow River. Located from Gansu Province to Hainan Province the Yangshao existed from 5000BC to 3000 BC.

The Yangshao culture was first discovered in 1921 by the Swedish archaeologist, Johan Gunnar Andersson. Found in Yangshuo Village in Henan Province more than 1,000 remains of Yangshao culture were found successively. Most of the discoveries were based in North China's Shaanxi Province showing a large and well travelled culture.

The Yangshao people grew rice and millet. They also farmed pigs, cattle and horses. The art of pottery making was also developed and refined. Excavated pottery shows us they knew how to paint, treat and process clay. Many of the remains look delicate and beautiful with painted animal and face designs.

The Longshan Culture
5000 to 4000 BC

The Longshan culture would overlap the Yangshao Culture and display many similar attributes. Most notably their knowledge on creating black pottery was superior to the Yangshao, with even more beautiful examples being found today.

From the fall of the Longshan culture there is a missing period of 2000 years in known history. What cultures or societies lived in this time remain a mystery. Overlooking speculation and imagination we can see that Chinese civilisation grew exponentially in the bronze age. These developments may have disturbed any remnants of archaeological evidence or naturally evolved from whatever happened in this missing era.

THE BRONZE AGE
3000 to 1200 BC

Many would say this is when Chinese Civilisation officially began. The reality is ancient Chinese society would only formalise and bridge many of the already established communities together in this time.

This led to the era of Dynasties, Clans and the earliest hint of a nation state. The five thousand years of pre-history had successfully laid the foundation for the next two thousand years of Dynasty rule.

THE EARLY DYNASTIES

The Xia Dynasty was long thought to be a myth, that was until archaeologists found the Shang Oracle Bones. These marked the acceptance of a civilisation which ran from 2070BC to 1600BC. The find of such bones was not ordinary, as the fragments are part animal and part turtle shell; All of which have ancient Chinese language inscriptions carved onto them.

To this day not all have been decoded and translated, but some don't need to be. Many of the words and symbols bare the exact same resemblance (and possible meaning) as language and words used in China today. Located in modern day Henan the number of excavations, developments and other same era societies (and their remnants) has allowed for a half painted picture and understanding of this Dynasty.

The considerable overlap of cultures has led many experts to question whether the settlements came under one ruler or several culturally similar chiefdoms. What is known is the civilisation concluded with the battle of Mingtaio and the decisive rise of the Shang Dynasty.

The Shang dynasty (1600 – 1046) was divided into two parts in time and location. The first of which was set in the Shang period, with settlement locations being at Erligang, Zhengzhou, and Shangcheng.

The second era is thought to have been in the Shang or Yin (殷) period, and found in modern day Henan. The Shang Dynasty had nine capitals and it is widely confirmed that modern day Henan was the final of these hubs.

Other records state the final Capital was in fact Yin, where the Dynasty moved in 1300BC. In total 31 Kings ruled the Shang Dynasty. With varying population numbers and common migrations it has led to the suspicion of whether it was in fact a separate entity or a merger between the former Xia Dynasty or later Yin Dynasty. The most common belief is the Dynasties of this time existed, co-operated and fought one another with overlapping time frames.

In light of this there was a definitive gap between these Dynasties and the next, named the Zhou dynasty. The Zhou Dynasty is believed to have remained in power from 1046 – 256 BC, making it the longest running and most continuous of all the ancient dynasties.

The Zhou Dynasty also led to the eradication and amalgamation of the Xia and Shang dynasty crossover period. They would ultimately be defeated at the Battle of Muye. Here the dynasty moved up the Yellow River Valley and

Eastward. The brothers and rulers of the Zhou, it's King and the Duke Wu proved themselves to the people through a mandate and initiation.

The won the territory and therefore control over Ancient China. They spread word of and implemented a new semi-feudalistic system. This innovation allowed for a decentralised rule and relied on on the culture believing they had come to power through this mandate by heaven.

This concept of a Heavenly Mandate which determined the ruler would take place in every succeeding Chinese Dynasty since. The mandate was not susceptible to a ruler losing power in an unworthy power grab or coup, being conquered by opposition or any other such outward reason. The only way an ancient ruler of a Dynasty could lose power was if they lost interest in their people.

If this occurred then a new House and ruler of the Dynasty would be granted the mandate of heaven. With several physical records that remain intact today they do not indicate that the Zhou ever experienced such events.

With a steady flow of inward migration and strong loyalty to the Dynasty the society moved up river over the course of their rule. The Dynasty began in now modern day Xi'an and slowly move all the way to South China.

THE IRON AGE

The beginning of the Iron Age in China is placed between the Autumn period between 722 – 476 BC and the Warring States period between 476 – 221 BC. Between these eras the old and formal Dynasties were undermined by bandit movements. Much of the Dynasties efforts were committed to fending off raids and developing as quickly as possible, to prevent chaos. As such both of the old dynasties went to war and several new ones emerged.

Much of the traditional folklore is set in this unstable but highly mystical era. Large parts of the nation were still untouched by civilisation. It is also where the modern term Shanzhai comes from, translating as 'mountain strongholds' it is now used when describing pirate groups and goods.

The Autumn Period, officially named the Spring and Autumn Period by historical records saw massive aggravation and conflict. The most prominent Dynasty of this time was the Zhou, who used their culture and soft power to expand. Local military leaders acted as soldier statesmen with oversight on all trade rather than militia or campaign driven warriors.

This led to new factions, cartels and nefarious offshoots from official business. Corruption would increase and in fact become an accepted aspect to the society. This Iron Age society continued to grow naturally up until the invasion of the North West, by the Qin People and Dynasty.

What followed was a subsequent relocation of the Zhou Capital to modern day Louyang. This began the new era of the Eastern Zhou and fall of the main Dynasty.

The military leaders became further distant from their Kings and fealty, becoming more like War Lords than military and political chiefs. The Dynasty had been broken into hundreds of different communities, all loyal their local war lord, which in more cases than not assumed a royal title.

By 600 BC the majority of these clans, communes or small states had been absorbed, amalgamated or simply died out. This era ran parallel and is often grouped in with the Warring States period, from 476 to 221 BC.

The Southern States remained largely independent. Their cultures were distinct and even amidst Wars with the North new cities developed. Slowly modern Chinese culture began to take shape and 'The Hundred Schools of Thought' and Chinese philosophy blossomed.

Confucianism, Taoism, Legalism and Mohism were founded, partly in response to the changing political world. Whilst this cultural and intellectual revolution went on so did the battles of the Warring States.

This era broke down into three pivotal moments;

x) After years of bloodshed, attempted coups and total war the three remaining and most powerful families of the Jin state set boundaries and partitioned the state. The families were the Zhao, Wei and Han.

x) Upon further political consolidation, seven prominent states remained by 500BC. The Zhou King would remain until 256 BC, but he was largely a figurehead and held no real power.

x) Areas of modern Sichuan and Liaoning were annexed, they were Governed under the new local administrative system of commandery and prefecture.

x) Ying Zheng, the king of Qin unified six powers and annexed the modern regions of Zhejiang, Fujian, Guangdong and Guangxi. This also made him the First Emperor of China (Qin Shi Huang).

The philosophers Laozi, Confucius and Sun Tzu all lived during this chaotic period. They would map the events and history through documentation.

IMPERIAL CHINA

Imperial China can be divided into three sub-periods:
Early, Middle, and Late.

The early period is notable for;

x) The Qin unification of China and their replacement by the Han.

x) The loss of Northern China.

x) The Jin Unification.

The Middle period was diverse. It encompassed the Sui unification, their supplementation by the Tang and the Song unification. All of this would lead to the emergence of the Yuan, Ming, and Qing dynasties.

The Qin Dynasty is believed to be the centre point and beginning of Imperial China. Under the first Emperors rule the Qin Dynasty subdued and formalised most of the Han Chinese Homeland under one empire.

The decline of Imperial China began after the fall of the Song and rise of the Mongol led Yuan Dynasty. Despite thriving as an Empire and leading onto two more semi successful dynasties the rule of Imperial China ended with the Qing Dynasty in 1912. Inevitably there is great deal of unknown history but the Dynastic rule still echoes across the modern nation.

In total 13 Great Dynasties ruled Ancient and Imperial China and by understanding them it becomes easier to see the parallels between modern and historical China, the cyclical nature of the land and how the national character and traits have become defined.

TIMELINE

XIA DYNASTY / 2070bc to 1600bc
SHANG DYNASTY / 166bc to 1050bc
ZHOU DYNASTY / 1046bc to 256bc

IMPERIAL CHINA

QIN DYNASTY / 221bc to 206bc

WESTERN HAN DYNASTY / 206bc to 220ad

XIN DYNASTY / 9ad to 23ad

EASTERN HAN / 25ad to 220ad

THE THREE KINGDOMS ERA / 220ad to 280ad

SIX DYNASTIES PERIOD / 220ad to 589ad

THE JIN DYNASTY / 266ad to 420ad

THE LIU SONG DYNASTY / 420ad – 479ad

THE NORTHERN TRIBES / 304ad to 600ad

THE NORTHERN AND SOUTHERN DYNASTIES / 420ad to 589ad

SUI DYNASTY / 581ad-618ad

TANG DYNASTY / 618ad-906ad

FIVE DYNASTIES PERIOD, TEN KINGDOMS / 907ad-960ad

SONG, LIAO, JIN AND WESTERN XIA DYNASTIES / 960ad to 1279ad

YUAN DYNASTY / 1279ad to 1368ad

MING DYNASTY / 1368ad to 1644ad

QING DYNASTY / 1644ad to 1912ad

QIN / CHI'IN DYNASTY

221bc to 202bc

Located in the Gansu and Shaanxi Provinces (near modern day Xi'an) the Qin Dynasty crushed six of the seven Warring States and the Zhou Dynasty.

In doing so it became the first Dynasty of Imperial China. It utilised a legalist system which resembled the structure of a totalitarian or fascist state, where dissidents, political enemies and opposition were eliminated. The Dynasty even employed strategies like book burning ceremonies and the burying of scholars. Those who were loyal to the Emperor rose in the regime and those who prevented further expansion went missing.

The Qin gave enormous power to the administrators, allowing Emperor Qin to focus on massive public works projects. Power was taken from the landowners and given to the peasantry. In doing so the Emperor implemented a near Communist level of control and empowerment of the working class.

This would lead to 300,000 peasants and convicts forming a colossal work force. They joined the Northern Great Wall of China, built a massive public road system and constructed the Emperors Mausoleum, guarded by a life size Terracotta Army for the dead Emperor.

The Emperor's tomb itself is yet to be excavated, but the main necropolis was found underneath a hill by two young boys in 1978. Since this time an entire underground palace, six hundred pits, 7000 Terracotta Statues, 100 wooden chariots and 20,000 square metres of the complex have been discovered. The rest of the structure is yet to be explored as modern technology is not yet capable of preserving the outer layers of the finds. Those items which have been excavated have denatured, with outer layers quickly peeling or crumbling. Having been underground for over 2000 years the Institutions protecting the site have put a hold on exploration and excavation, that is until technology and method have improved significantly.

Located in Modern Day Xinjiang the Qin Dynasty evolved into a heavily legalistic and bureaucratic system early on. It's huge entrance gates marked the first real entry point into old China for those on the silk road. The origins of the name China can also be traced to the Qin Dynasty, with Qin sounding like 'Chin' when pronounced.

With 90 percent of the Qin Dynasty being classed as peasantry the leaders did well to empower them. By using the Southward expansion and conflicts with the other Dynasties the Qin Peasants quickly gained wealth and private assets.

When the Emperor died the once loyal bureaucrats fought for power. The Empire would fall a few short years later. Even with the Qin Dynasties contributions to China and it's stability a counter movement was formed.

The ethnic Han people and the Han Dynasty would rise with the collapse of the Qin and bring a softer system of political governance. This allowed for the Qin Dynasty (and their burial sites) to largely be forgotten about as the generations passed.

Contributions of the Qin Dynasty include -

Arithmetic, centralized government, the unification and development of the legal code, written language, measurement, the currency of China, standards and regulations (for example production, trade and services), taxation and the connection of the Northern border walls in turn creating first Great Wall of China.

Qin Dynasty

WESTERN HAN DYNASTY
202bc to 9ad

The Han dynasty remains to this day the most famous of the Chinese Dynasties. Many modern Chinese are direct descendants of the Han, sharing the same names as those who lived in this era.

The first Han dynasty would come to be known as the Western Han, but the Han Empire and people would rise and decline in several different eras.

As the Western Han Dynasty bought stability for such a long duration it is considered to be a Golden Age of China. Areas under the Han's control (a large part of Eastern, Central and Western China today) progressed to new levels of societal achievement.

The foundations of the Han Dynasty took over what was once Qin territory. They did so by unifying the regions which had become separated under an Imperial Democracy. This more liberal style of Governance led to huge developments in art, culture and science, with Confucianism becoming a popular belief.

Both language and mathematics flourished as well. Parts of modern Chinese (Mandarin) language were forged and Mathematics was practically created.

The greatest achievement of this Dynasty was not in it's creation of thought or equations but it's most famous leader. The first Emperors, Wen and Jing adopted a stand-backish approach to managing the Empire. They saw it grow organically where as Emperor Wu, (the most notable leader) bought the Dynasty into what could have been the most advanced of all the worlds civilisations at the time.

He doubled the size of the Empire and employed a strict legalist system whilst encouraging Confucianism at all levels of society. He also pursued successful military campaigns against the Xiongnu Empire and the Baiyue tribes.

Under his rule the The Han also;

x) Annexed Minyue in 135 BC and 111 BC, Nanyue in 111 BC, and Dian in 109 BC.

x) Led cultural expeditions South which expedited assimilation and partnership with the Empires of South East Asia.

x) Reduced influence North of the Great Wall with the diplomatic efforts of Zhang Qian.

x) Influenced the states of the Tarim Basin to better themselves.

x) Opened up the Silk Road that connected China to the West.

The Fall of the Dynasty

The Dynasty would ultimately fall to bandits and greedy Lords after the death of Emperor Wu. The Han resurged with the rise of Wang Mang, the Xin Dynasty, the era of the Six Dynasties, the short lived Eastern Han and arguably to this very day, - with the vast majority of Chinese Nationals being ethnic Han.

THE XIN DYNASTY

9ad to 23ad

In 9ad Wang Mang took control of the remnants of the Han Dynasty. Acknowledging the Mandate from Heaven he declared and worked toward the total fall of the Han and rise of the Xin.

In doing so he won loyalty through security and built the Xin Dynasty, which was short lived but important for China as a whole. Uniquely, many supporters of Wang Mang, the Xin and it's policies were once Han loyalists.

The Xin Dynasty under Wang Mang outlawed slavery and redistributed private lands to the public. In doing so he lost favour with the landholding families and set the grounds for the mob to dictate rule. This combined with mass flooding of the redistributed farmlands led to the murder of Wang Mang by an enraged peasant mob. After his death the Xin Dynasty collapsed and the Easter Han Dynasty rose to power.

THE EASTERN HAN DYNASTY

25ad–220ad

The Eastern Han Dynasty was the Second Imperial Dynasty of China. The Emperor Guangwu rose to power and bought with him the ethos of the Western Han Dynasty.

This resurgence forever shaped China. Landholding and merchant families, as well as the peasant folk all supported the shift back to Han rule and the former model of society. The new capital was located at Luoyang, East of the former capital Xi'an.

The empire flourished with the creation of papermaking by Cai Lun, the numerous scientific and mathematical contributions by the famous polymath Zhang Heng and development of metallurgy, taxation, astronomy, cartography, medicine and engineering all fortified the dynasty.

Eastern Han Society actively supported the Emperors Guangwu, Ming and Zhang, all of which were brilliant administrators. They led succesful military campaigns against the Xiongnu Empire and even reopened the silk road.

A Diplomat, Scholar and military General named Ban Chao even led conquests across the Pamirs to the Caspian Sea. This enabled Buddhism to enter the Dynasty alongside Diplomatic missions with the Ancient Romans.

Ancient Rome is even recorded as having established two embassies within the Eastern Han empire in 166ad and 284ad.

THE THREE KINGDOMS
220ad – 280ad

By 220ad Three Kingdoms had emerged after years of conflict and instability. The fall of the Eastern Han led to Clans and Warlords fighting for dominance under the Yellow Turban Rebellion in 184ad.

This created a nation wide demand for structure and peace. By 208ad the leader named Cao Cao unified the North of China. It would be his son who formalised and created the Wei Dynasty in 220ad. This would mark the beginning of the era's Three Kingdoms.

The other two Kingdoms were formed by two opposition clans, which had declared their own independence. They would form the Shu and Wu empires.

The creation of three separate Kingdoms all opposed to one another led to several more decades of chaos. The structure and stability of the former Han Dynasties had been done and the power of the Xin forgotten entirely.

The era of sporadic militia fighting, quests, adventurers and instability has been romanticized over time. It is the time where many of China's greatest myths and legends were set and even created.

The Jin Dynasty would conquer the Northern Wei Dynasty and unify the whole nation in 280ad.

SIX DYNASTIES
220ad-589ad

The Six Dynasties is an umbrella term used for the Han regimes which ruled empires from the years 220ad to 589ad. The dynasties faced an overlap in timeframe with both the Three Kingdoms and Jin Dynasty.

They were based in South China and close to the Yangzi river. Culture flourished and Buddhism took hold of the communities. In conjunction to this the arts advanced at a tremendous rate.

The capital of the true Dynasties were located in modern day Nanjing, then known as Jianking. This makes it the only era in Chinese History when the capital was located in South China.

They Six dynasties were;
x The Eastern Wu
x The Eastern Jin
x The Liu Song
x The Southern Qi
x The Liang Dynasty
x The Chen Dynasty

THE JIN DYNASTY
266ad – 420ad

The Jin dynasty defeated the Wei and held power in two distinct distinct domains. These were the Eastern and Western Jin. The Jin were in effect several empires that amalgamated under one banner and one ethnic majority to take control of China.

The Jin Dynasty would go onto fight numerous opposition forces in the North, namely against the ethnic Mongol, Turkic and Tibetan tribes. The Jin Dynasty was also subject to several power struggles by Princes seeking sole power. These factors led to instability and the polar opposite of why they had formed.

This all led to the two domains of the Dynasty fracturing and forming opposing Dynasties. This was concurrent to the rise of the Former Qin

Dynasty of 351ad to 394ad. The Former Qin Dynasty would conquer Western Jin first and then take control of all other tribal regions in 376ad.

The former Qin would collapse after defeat and internal rebellions in 394ad before they could take the Eastern Jin, which would survive for 26 more years. As the North dissolved into a series of clan run independent realms the Thai, Tibetan and other Northern Tribes all proved troublesome to the Jin Empire.

The Jin, despite harbouring some of the best academics in History the Dynasty would fall to several military led coups. These destabilised the dynasty and allowed for the final revolutionary, a man named Liu Yu to take power. He murdered the Emperor Gong, the penultimate Jin Dynasty emperor and forced his brother to abdicate the inherited throne. Once in power Liu Yu formed and became the first emperor of the Liu Song Southern Dynasty.

THE NORTHERN TRIBES (WU-HU)
304ad - 600ad

South China was practically a different civilisation when compared to the North during this time. The North had already experienced the rise and fall of several Dynasties and several tribes and clans all fought for power. The disconnected and nomadic nature of these clans even began to indicate toward the rise of the Mongol Empire, which would form 1400 years later.

It was the former Qin Dynasty from 351ad to 394ad which was the most prolific of the Northern Tribes. This Qin dynasty had taken inspiration and been founded upon the same grounds as the First Qin Dynasty. It united all 16 of the Eastern Kingdoms and established it's capital in Xi'an. The dynasty was successful in conquering the Western Jin and all other Northern Tribes.

It would only collapse when it's leader Fu Jian died in 385ad. The name 'Wu-Hu' was a collective name for all the wild and largely nomadic Northern tribes. Whilst most of the Tribes within the state borders of modern China joined the former Qin the tribes of Mongolia and the North Eastern Ordos region refused.

For their refusal to join and formalise under the former Qin Dynasty these tribes were deemed a threat and had a trade ban placed on them. The ban was enforced at all levels which led the Xiongnu tribe, based in the Ordos region to frequently raid the former Qin Dynasty.

After several skirmishes and small battles the former Qin declared War on the Xiongnu. The Qin General Meng Tian and his forces conquered the territory in 215 BC and quickly established new agricultural settlements.

This was the first real victory of the former Qin and unified Northern Tribes. However the North West region was not kept as the culturally distinct Ordos region proved to wild or too unwilling to join the other Northern Chinese Tribes as a Dynasty.

The region would in fact become a breeding ground for dissidents, militias and failed territory management scenarios, for both the Qin Dynasty and later Han Dynasty; Both of which would gain power over the region but lose it due to peasant rebellions, overpopulation and resource depletion.

The wild nature and culture of the tribes which made up the Former Qin Dynasty would ultimately become their downfall. After a failed campaign against the Jin and several internal rebellions the Qin collapsed and soon returned to a Northern structure of independent tribes for 150 years.

The Northern regions of the 5th and 6th century soon resembled their former selves before the Qin and collective agreements. Even more non-Chinese and nomadic settlers moved to the North and would remain in the area until this very day.

These ethnic Mongol or Turkic people would strengthen the now independent and nomadic tribes. They would go onto became 'the five barbarians,' the five Wu or five tribes named the Xiongnu, Jie, Xianbei, Di, and Qiang.

THE LIU SONG DYNASTY
420ad – 479ad

The Southern Song Dynasty, otherwise known as the Liu Song Dynasty rose to power in an aggressive fashion. This aggressive nature was sustained throughout it's short lifespan of 59 years.

It's founder, Liu Yu died two years into the Dynasty which led to a line of brutal and blood thirsty rulers. Emperors of the Liu Song were amongst some of the nastiest in all China's history. The base line of this viscousness was set by Emperor Ming, the 11th Son of the then Emperor. He would come to power and execute all male family members and heirs to the throne.

It is this viscousness displayed in the Dynasties leaders which caused peasant uprisings and the Dynasties destruction. Being so far south the Dynasty was out of reach from the Northern Tribes and would make up part of the Southern Dynasty.

The Liu Song, despite it's problems did have a lasting influence on the culture and image of Southern China. Many of the traits we imagine when thinking about Souther China were progressed and formed in this age.

NORTHERN AND SOUTHERN DYNASTY
420ad – 589ad

In the early 5th century as the Northern tribes disbanded China entered a period known as the Northern and Southern dynasties. It was in this age when Imperial China bore the same traits as a nation engaged in civil war.

The opposing regimes ruled both the northern and southern halves of the country, despite the fact they did not go to total war with one another the division of the nation led to cultural progression. By command of the people society continued to progress and personal development encouraged. Buddhism was taken up as the most popular belief system and Taoism became the most common philosophical and spiritual credence.

Both schools of thought would be accepted and coexist. Despite a lack of structure, Government or system in place public opinion and thinking took communities y storm. After many years of intolerance and conflict over ideology it would take this era to bring some level of peace, at least in mainland and southern China.

The attributes of the North really took shape too. Northern Tribes after the fall of the former Qin dynasty became even more like their projected image of savage and nomadic barbarians. Even with the tyrannical leaders of the South society fostered honour, culture, discipline and decency amongst the inhabitants.

The South had several distinct stages to it, where as the North was more or less a constant. This can be seen in the leadership and overlap of formal Dynasties. The South was led and termed the Eastern Jin, which would give way to the Liu Song, the Southern Qi, the Liang and finally Chen dynasties. Each of the dynasties were short lived but ruled by ethnic Han families.

They used defensive measures and strategy to fend off attacks from the North. This allowed them to preserve many aspects of the former Chinese civilizations, even with peasant rebellions and the Dynasties falling.

This attribute also started one of the first real culture wars. When the Northern Tribes returned to their historical structure of being disintegrated and nomadic they would eventually be moulded by the South. By adopting the culture, skills and values of the South they would eventually Sinify.

The 16 tribal Kingdoms of the North did not fall after the former Jin's collapse or fight themselves into extinction, they would fall via cultural appropriation.

Traditionally the Northern Tribes were Mongol or Turkic, but as the Southern Dynasties grew so did this sinofication. Soon the tribal leaders partnered with Ethnic Han until the two had assimilated with Han offspring taking full control of the North.

The most notable example of this is in the Northern Wei who formed the Xianbei Kingdom. They would amalgamate the Northern Tribes over time and soon adopted Han surnames, customs and traditions.

SUI DYNASTY
581ad-618ad

The short-lived Sui dynasty was an essential period in Chinese history. Founded by THE Emperor Wen in 581ad it would go onto unify China, conquering the Southern Chen and concluding three centuries of political division.

The Sui pioneered and launched new institutions, including the government system of Three Departments and Six Ministries. They also reduced the weight of a good blood line and hereditary power.

This can be seen in the following Sui projects and policies;

X Allowing commoners to become officials via strict Imperial examinations.

X Improving the fubing militia system and conscription.

X Introducing the equal-field system or land-equalization sytem to manage land distribution amongst the people.

X Creating standardized coinage.

X Openness to Buddhism and using it in conjunction with Taoism.

The Mega Construction Projects

X The Grand Canal development for shipping grain and troops to the Capitals of Daxing (Chang'an) and Luoyang. Shipments were also sent to the wealthy South East region and North East border.

X The Great Wall was also expanded on a massive scale to defend the Dynasty from the Northern Tribes and Kingdoms.

SUI FALL

The Sui were responsible for a great deal of good and bringing peace to a time of turmoil. The dynasty suppressed counter movements, rebels and criminals - both within and outside it's borders. The Dynasty would fall with it's expansion North into the Korean Peninsula. The mass invasions and military defeats of the Goguryeo–Sui War caused an internal uprising which would collapse the whole dynasty.

Sui Dynasty

TANG DYNASTY

618ad – 907ad

The Tang dynasty and it's legacy are still prominent in culture today, despite the communist revolution and more than a thousand years of change. These factors alone ought to have reduced the memory and heritage of the Tang to history books alone, the fact that it remains a popular inspiration is a powerful testament to it's place in China's history.

The dynasty was founded by Emperor Gaozu in 618ad. It soon became a golden age of Chinese civilization and microclimate for positive development. It is now largely understood to have been the most prosperous period of ancient China, with significant developments in culture, art, literature, poetry and technology.

Buddhism became the predominant religion for the common people, which then started to mark the decline in the folk and tribal religions. The national capital Chang'an, now modern day Xi'an was the largest city in the world during its time.

The second Emperor of the Tang Dynasty, Taizong, is widely regarded as one of the greatest emperors in all of China's history. He laid the foundation for the dynasty to flourish for centuries, long after his own reign.

A combination of military conquests and diplomatic manoeuvrers;
X Eliminated the threats from nomadic tribes.
X Extended the border.

X Submitted neighbouring states into a tributary system.

This was instrumental to the rise of the dynasty which allowed for the soft power, cultural progressions and economic prosperity which followed.

As the Empire expanded several military victories in the Tarim Basin kept the Silk Road open. This connected Chang'an to Central Asia and areas far to the West.

In the south, lucrative maritime trade routes opened from the port cities such as Guangzhou. There was extensive trade with distant lands and empires. Many foreign merchants would settle in China during this time which built a cosmopolitan and diverse culture. This era also marks the beginning of the largely under studied history of pirates in Ancient China.

The Tang culture and social systems were observed and replicated in neighbouring countries, most notably, Japan, Cambodia and Thailand. Within the Tang the central canal linked the political heartland in Chang'an to the agricultural and economic centres in the East and South.

A large part of the dynasties success was due to the strong centralized bureaucracy, which acted on effective policies. The government was organized as "Three Departments and Six Ministries" like the Sui Dynasty.

The offices would draft, review and implement policies. It was comprised of both officials and land owning families. This gave perspective, intelligence and experience to the policies, which is what really made them a success.

The Tang dynasty also introduced an "equal-field system" where all land was owned by the Emperor and granted to people according to household size. Families granted land would offer a male, (the son or father) for conscripted military service for a fixed period each year. This was developed from the fubing system of previous dynasties.

The policy stimulated rapid growth in the military forces and assisted in the dynasties productivity. This early form of reservist or territorial army offered both a significant level of professional soldiers, without straining the state treasury.

As with all policies there were loopholes and by the dynasty's midpoint the full time, standing army had replaced the reservist conscription. The once semi public farms and land were taken back into private ownership and senior officials sought to increase their own power.

In light of this the dynasty continued to flourish. The Tang dynasty is often associated with the only Empress Regnant in Chinese history. Her name was Wu Zetian and under her rule the Tang dynasty stretched from the Pacific to the Aral Sea, with at least 50 million subjects.

Empress Wu Zetian was an effective leader, albeit power hungry and truly brutal. She began her career in the court of the Tang Dynasty as an Imperial Consort and slowly rose up the hierarchy, via elimination of competition and Machiavellian stance on power.

Her rule acted as the zenith of prosperity of the empire. Despite several occupations, rebellions and counter movements the Tang Dynasty under the Empress continued to develop.

However administrative negligence in times of conflict undermined the strong rule, which would eventually lead to the collapse of the empire. The Imperial Government was far from the once well run and formerly active system it had once been.

Opinion amongst the regional leaders soon changed from fealty and loyalty to ambition and greed. As rebellions continued to rock the society the taxes and reliance on Dynasty managed business increased. This all led to regional military governors, known as Jiedushi taking up a more active role in the society. They too became ambitious and took advantage of the weakened Tang Dynasty.

The border territories soon fell to these leaders, who were now more similar to Warlords in command of bandit armies. In spite of this the civil society of the Tang Dynasties central regions continued to progress, even without the protection or structure of a Government.

The final years of the Dynasty can be marked between the Huang Chao Rebellion, from 874ad to 884ad and Zhu Wen's usurpation. The Huang Chao Rebellion would devastate the entire empire for a decade.

The rebellion peaked with the sacking of the southern port city of Guangzhou in 879AD. Almost all of the inhabitants had been massacred and the large foreign merchant enclaves were looted, pillaged and destroyed.

Three years later in 881ad, both Capital Cities, Luoyang and Chang'an fell.

Any loyal members of the Imperial Government had gone into hiding or became corrupt. Huge reliance was placed on the ethnic Han and Turkic warlords in suppressing the rebellions. Most would ultimately betray the Empire and use their power strategically to increase their lands and influence. The end of the era and collapse of the Dynasty is marked by Zhu Wen's usurpation and following years of national division.

Tang Dynasty

FIVE DYNASTIES AND TEN KINGDOMS
907ad – 960ad

The short period of political disunity between the Tang and the Song Dynasty came to be known as the Five Dynasties and Ten Kingdoms period. It lasted from 907ad to 960ad and for fifty three years ancient China was a fractured and multi-state system.

The remnants of the Tang dynasty would resurface or be taken over by the five regimes, all of which were replica states of previously successful Dynasties.

The five dynasties were;
X The Later Liang
X The Later Tang
X The Later Jin
X The Later Han
X The Later Zhou

Each dynasty overlapped and in turn succeeded one another. The base of the dynasties and their activities were centralised to the Chinese heartland, thus creating a new centre of Imperial China.

The rulers and population of the Later Tang, Jin and Han were Chinese by nature. Their values, customs and traditions were focused on the older dynasties and bringing about a popular resurgence.

There were several times in these Dynasties when non ethnic Chinese, notably descendants of the tribal Shatuo Turks ruled over an ethnic majority of Han Chinese. Over time they too underwent sinofication.

In the South and West of China the Ten Kingdoms emerged. There were in fact dozens of independent states which ran concurrently to the main Five Dynasties. The factions and clans created by the Warlords of the former Tang dynasty had simply formalised and maintained their positions. The majority were ethnic Han and despite the division there was relative peace.

The Ten Kingdoms of this era were the; Yang Wu, Wuyue, Min, Southern Han, Ma Chu, Northern Han, Jingnan or Nanping, Former Shu, Later Shu and the Southern Tang.

Whilst they may seem like a small part of Chinese History the Five Dynasties and Ten Kingdoms would become a pivotal aspect to China's unification by the Song. The nature of the smaller states allowed for the Zhou General Zhao Kuangy to lead a coup, which in fact led to the annihilation of the Ten Kingdoms.

The lasting legacies of this era are;
X The now famous varied landscape paintings of Ancient China, it's mountains, woodlands and natural areas.

41

X White paint and design in Ceramics and Pottery.

X Vietnam gained lasting independence after being a Chinese prefecture for many centuries.

SONG, LIAO, JIN AND WESTERN XIA DYNASTIES
960ad – 1279ad

In the year 960ad the Song dynasty was founded by Emperor Taizu. The capital was established in Kaifeng, also known as Bianjing. In 979ad the Song dynasty reunified most of the China proper, while large swaths of the outer territories were occupied by the non ethnic Chinese. These barbarian tribes would eventually be sinocized and become subservient to the Song.

The Liao Dynasty or Khitan Liao dynasty lasted from 907 to 1125. It ruled over large parts of Northern China, including Manchuria and Mongolia.

In the same time the Western Xia Dynasty began to form. It would take hold properly from 1032 to 1227 in what is now the North Western Chinese provinces of Gansu, Shaanxi and Ningxia.

The Tangut tribes were prominent founders of the Western Xia dynasty. It quickly became clear that to become a prominent power they would have to replicate the Jin Dynasty and recover the strategic Sixteen Kingdoms.

The Southern Song Dynasty soon went to War with the Northern Liao Dynasty. The Song launched several major campaigns against the Northern Liao in the early years of this era. All of ended in failure.

During the Liao Dynasty counter campaign of 1004ad their heavy cavalry conquered the exposed North China Plain. They would go onto reach the outskirts of Kaifeng.

In doing so they forced the Song Dynasty into submission. What followed was an early agreement called the Chanyuan Treaty. It imposed heavy annual tributes from the Song treasury to the Liao in return for peace.

The Treaty would come to be known as symbol of extortion, barbarianism, anti-Imperialism and anti-Legalism. It also reversed the historical Chinese tributary system which devalued it within the Song.

This system of buying peace would continue and strategically turn in favour of the Song. The historical examples of the Southern culture war and gradual sinofication were utilised once again.
The annual outflow of Song silver to the Liao was paid back through the purchase of Chinese goods and products. This expanded the Song economy, replenished its treasury and increased foot traffic and soft power connections with the North. It also dampened the appetite for War amongst citizens of he Song and proved a strong incentive to better relationships with the Liao.

In addition to the cross-border trade and contact the stories of the Song and it's culture soon reached the Northern Liao. Most of the Liao subjects were hardened farmers, hunters, nomads. The Empire covered Northern and North Eastern China, Mongolia and parts of North Korea and the Russian Far East.

The further North the harder the life, so tales of the Southern Climate, lifestyle, cuisine and culture spread rapidly. Soon Southward migrations began and in turn much of the Song Culture was embraced. In turn, the Song Dynasty also adopted many of the Liao perspectives in this time, specifically towards the freedom of Women.

Song-Liao Women
Song women were confined to societal boundaries with strict rules on their virginity, partners, roles and character. They were very much forced into subservient positions to the family or their husband and could never progress.

Liao women, by comparison were free. If their husbands were conscripted into military service it was their duty to manage the household, finances, farming duties and go hunting.

This led to a unique culture of many Song women, most notably Han Chinese becoming willing abductees to Liao men. In doing so they would consent to being taken as a trophy and engage in sexual activities before

43

marriage, which was punishable in the Song. More often than not they would then return home and be married.

Equally the cases of Han women being captured without their consent by raiding Liao or Liao bandits was high. This was the polar opposite of the above scenario with rape and enslavement taking place. In both cases of women heading North it led to the same outcome for the Song, the genetic lineage of their offspring and culture of the Han Chinese slowly took control.

Song-Jin Relations

A similar style of peace treaty and social-economical consequences can be found in the Song's relations with the Jin dynasty. The Jin Dynasty was established within the Liao by the Jurchen tribes.

They had revolted against their overlords in the Liao to establish the empire in 1115ad. The Jin took the extreme warrior culture of the Liao to a new level. By 1125ad the devastating Jin Cataphract (a form of heavily armoured cavalryman) annihilated the Liao dynasty.

Remnants of the Liao Court and it's surviving members fled to Central Asia and commenced the Qara Khitai Empire or Western Liao dynasty. The culture of Han and Song became more prevalent in this time.

The Jin soon disregarded the Treaty with the Song and invaded. By 1127ad Kaifeng was sacked and the massive catastrophe known as the Jingkang Humiliation took place. The Jin had taken control of the Capital and taken the Emperor, his family and court officials as prisoners.

This marked the end of the Northern Song and beginning of the Southern Song. Members of the Imperial family, notably a man named Zhao Gou would escape to South China. These surviving members of Song court regrouped in the new capital city of Hangzhou and Zhao Gou became Emperor Gaozong.

In this time the Western Xia Dynasty had formed and managed to avoid war with the Song, Jin and former Liao dynasties. Comprised of Nomads the Dynasty was also known as the Tangut Empire. The people were mainly traders and farmers and culturally distinct. The now extinct Tangut language was common, but the people were ethnically diverse with Tibetan, Han, Burmese and central Asian language and culture being present.

The closest allies to the Western Xia were in central Asia, so much of the trade and migrations went West, rather than into China proper. Soon the Dynasty, with it's reliable trade and use of the Silk road built two elite military units.

Known as the Iron Hawks (tie yaozi) and Trekker infantry (bubazi), or mountain infantry the dynasty pioneered new strategy. They would go onto integrate cavalry, chariots, archery, shields, artillery (cannons carried on the back of camels), and amphibious troops for combat on land and water. Had the forces been larger then they could have prevented the destruction of the Dynasty by the Invading Mongol armies. The scale of the Mongol Conquest was undefeatable which led to the Western Xia Dynasty joining the Mongol empire, after much of their culture and cities had been ransacked.

The Western Xia Dynasty did ask the Jin for assistance in the early conflicts with the Mongol forces. Stating it was not just for the preservation of the Western Xia Dynasty but the defence of China proper. The Jin would refuse which led to Western Xia joining and leading the Mongol conquest of the Jin Dynasty in 1234ad.

The Southern Song dynasty would defend against Mongol invasions for another 62 years, only falling to the Grandson of Ghenghis Khan and height of the Mongol Empire.

Song Dynasty

THE SONG DYNASTY - SOUTHERN SONG
1127ad–1279ad

Despite several military defeats and a projected image of weakness the Song is considered to be the high point of Imperial China. It is a pillar of classical Chinese civilisation which encompassed the best aspects of previous dynasties.

Despite the rise and fall of the Song from 960ad to 1276ad it is in the Southern and Final era of the Song where it's true potential was realised, only to fall to the Mongols soon after.

The reasons for the Song Dynasty being held in such high regard are numerous. It's spirit, society and soft power were world changing. It was the first place in World History to issue paper bank notes, use gunpowder and undergo an economic revolution.

As such the social life of the average citizen flourished, the population's education level increased with the distribution of publishing (made possible with innovating on the woodblock printing press.)

Alongside these innovations and new Government reform the Song reached a level of sophistication probably unseen in world history before this time. The Southern Song was founded by remnants of the Northern Song who implemented far more dramatic policies for the good of the people.

Enormous social movements were soon established, which led to further inward migrations and the progression of social districts in the cities. Theatre, opera, festivals and art shows soon became the norm, which in turn changed public thought. Confucian with a deep reliance on Buddhism became the norm, which in turn changed society even further.

Farming communities soon established their own administrators, grassroot movements and authorities for market standards. All of this led to an enormous rise in the population which surpassed 100 million people.

As standard of life for the working class improved it increased the Song's desirability by those outside it's borders, most notably in the eyes of the Mongols.

Innovation in rice cultivation and coal production also fuelled massive industrial developments. The capital cities, named Kaifeng and subsequently Hangzhou were both the most populous cities in the world at the time.

Although the land trading routes to the far West and North were blocked by nomadic empires, the Song traded extensively with neighbouring states via the ocean. Well established maritime trade routes and merchanting bought the Song all they needed for further growth. The Silk Road was also active and the Song coinage and paper notes were made the de facto currency.

Some of the creations and developments of this time are beyond imaginable. For instance, giant wooden vessels equipped with compasses travelled throughout the China Seas and northern Indian Ocean. These vessels were less like traditional ships and more like modern day apartment buildings.

Being multi levelled and immense in size they were used for exploration, warfare and trade. These secured Song ocean prominence and allowed for them to create the first standing Navy in China.

The concept of insurance was also practised by merchants in the Song, which in turn fuelled riskier expeditions and trade. This connected the Dynasty with merchants outside of Central Asia, Ancient Rome and Europe. Soon resources and goods were being taken from Africa and South East Asia as the Song traders hedged the risks of a long-haul maritime shipments through insurance. All of this in turn stimulated further economic growth and the first ever economy based on a tertiary sector boomed.

The western city of Chengdu was the first to entirely adopt paper currency. The Song Administration would go onto supplement and eventually replace huge quantities of copper coins with paper notes across the Dynasty.

In direct correlation to the economic advancements the Southern Song soon became the Chinese Golden Age for great advancements in science and technology. Inventions like the first hydro-mechanical astronomical clock, woodblock printing and paper money were created within the Dynasty.

The Song Court built on the principles learnt from the past Dynasties. They employed capable administrators with a variety of personal and professional backgrounds. This in turn led to two main groupings, the political reformers and the conservatives. It was led by the chancellors Wang Anshi and Sima Guang, respectively.

With Government support enormous literary works were compiled and catalogued in libraries during the Song dynasty. Historical work such as the Zizhi Tongjian or "Comprehensive Mirror to Aid in Government" were preserved and used as reference, much like Case Law in the West.

The Song dynasty also led military innovation and altered the course of warfare. Gunpowder was invented in the Tang dynasty but first used in conflict by the Song, which inspired new firearms, cannon's and siege engine designs.

The Southern Song and it's future were dependant on the protection of the Yangtze and Huai River. If the cavalry forces of the north took the Rivers the Song would be forced into submission.

This, alongside the protection of trade routes led to the first standing navy in China in 1132ad. They used Paddle-wheel warships equipped with trebuchet's. These could launch incendiary bombs at the shores, coastal cities and even other ships. These ships are recorded as being used in the Song's victory over the invading Jin forces at the Battle of Tangdao in the East China Sea, and the Battle of Caishi, on the Yangtze River in 1161.

The advances of the civilization stopped almost as abruptly as the empire itself. The devastating Mongol conquests reduced population numbers, forced an economic downfall and led to cultural discouragement.

These conditions would last for thirty years with Mongol invasions being fought off until the Song capital Hangzhou fell in 1276. The final annihilation of the Song was in the Battle of Yamen in 1279, when the military forces and navy were defeated. The following years led to mass suicides, famine and any hint of a resurgence leading to mass executions and increased Mongol military occupation.

YUAN DYNASTY – THE MONGOL EMPIRE
1271ad – 1368ad

The Yuan dynasty was proclaimed in 1271 by the grandson of Genghis Khan. His name was Kublai Khan, Great Khan of Mongol. He had assumed the additional title of Emperor of China after the fall of the Southern Song.

The Mongols conquered the Jin dynasty in Northern China several decades before the creation of the Yuan. The Southern Song dynasty then fell in 1279ad after a protracted and bloody war.

The Mongol ruled Yuan Dynasty became the first conquest dynasty in Chinese history to rule the entirety of China proper. The Yuan embraced all ethnicities within the empire, but the ruling population were rarely non ethnic Mongol.

The Yuan dynasty would also control the Mongolian heartland and other regions, inheriting the largest share of territory of all the divided Mongol Empire. The other Khanates were more Westward facing and consisted of;

The Golden Hoard (ruling 6,000,000 km2 of central Asia, from Northern Mongolia to modern day Hungary and Poland.)

The Chagatai Khanate (ruling over 3,500,000 km2 of modern day Tibet, Northern India, Pakistan, Nepal, Myanmar.)

The Ilkhanate (ruling over 3,750,000 km2 of modern day Iran, Azerbaijan, Turkey, Iraq, Armenia, Georgia, Afghanistan, Turkmenistan, Pakistan, Dagestan and Tajikistan.

The Yuan was accepted as the Empire of the Great Khan and it's Emperors of as the nominal Great Khan (Khagan) of the greater Mongol Empire. They gained supremacy over the other Mongol Khanates, all of which acknowledged the Yuan as the top Sovereign.

The yuan soon tried for further expansion South and East, but were halted after defeats in the invasions of Japan and Vietnam.

Following the previous example of the Jin dynasty, the capital of the Yuan was established in Khanbaliq, also known as Dadu, now known as modern-day Beijing.

The Grand Canal was reconstructed and connected the remote capital to former Song economic hubs in the South. This centralised the city and laid the foundations for Beijing to remain as the capital of the nation state forever.

This era would come to be known as Pax Mongolica, where the whole of the Asian continent would grow close to the Mongol Empire or be directly under their rule. For the first and only time in history, the silk road connecting East and West was controlled by a single state. This led to improved infrastructure, security, flow of people, trade, and the cultural exchange.

The network of roads grew and a postal system was even established. This all further connected the Empire which would become the largest Empire in Human History when it came to a consecutive and connected landmass.

The remnants of the Song Dynasties maritime trade were salvaged and developed. Soon sea routes and ocean based trade flourished. Quanzhou and Hangzhou would emerge as the largest ports in the world.

In this era travellers from the far west, most notably the Venetian, Marco Polo settled in China for decades. Respectively travellers from the Far East also travelled West and setup the very first Chinese settlements, which eventually grew into the largest cities China Town's.

As such the detail of travel records, stories, tales, experiences and knowledge increased through the travel of these people. They would go onto inspire many generations of medieval Europeans and Yuan inhabitants to continue trade and the flow of goods between East and West.

The Yuan Dynasty also implemented a structure where paper currency alone could be used across the Empire, becoming the first world empire to do so.

This lack of tangible coin or asset reliance in fact led to hyperinflation, which would influence the eventual downfall.
The Fall of the Yuan
The fall of the Yuan was monumental and due to 4 reasons; The Yuan Mongols had become too Chinese and were rejected by the other Khanates. Hyperinflation caused an economic collapse. Racial Politics and never viewing the Han as Leaders would take a toll and the rise of the Ming and Yuan failure in never really eradicating the loyalty and memory of the Song.

Before the Mongol invasion China's population was recorded at 120 million. By the end of the conquest it was down to 60 million. Throughout the Yuan dynasty there was general sentiment among the populace against the Mongol dominance. Thousands of ethnic Han were conscripted into the

Hoards to fight. Their children were forced into the earliest form of Public Schools and whilst this bred a strong military and administration it undermined all loyalty.

The surface loyalty was never to the Mongol leadership, but rather to stability. As the Khanate and administration weakened the fractures and disloyalty grew. Soon the largest and most widespread peasant uprisings since the 1340s took place.

The Yuan Dynasty and Chinese Mongol Empire would fall after the massive naval engagement at Lake Poyang, as part of the Red Turban Rebellion. Here Zhu Yuanzhang destroyed the rebel forces in the South and proclaimed himself emperor of the Ming Dynasty in 1368.

That same year his northern expedition army captured the capital Khanbaliq and ended Mongol rule over China proper. The remnants of the Yuan Dynasty fled North, back to Mongolia and sustained the regime. From this point the other Mongol Khanates of Central Asia would continue to exist, but eventually all would fall from power.

Yuan Dynasty

MING DYNASTY
1368ad – 1644ad

The Ming dynasty was founded in 1368 by Zhu Yuanzhang. He led China against the Mongol-Yuan Dynasty who he would ultimately defeat. With the collapse of the Yuan Empire Zhu Yuanzhang would suppress several rebellions and offer hope of a new era during times of plague and famine. He won the loyalty of the nation and soon proclaimed himself as the Hongwu Emperor, under a special mandate of heaven.

Khanbaliq was still a hub of Yuan loyalists so the South and newly established Ming would march on this city, now the modern day capital of China.

After winning control the Ming Dynasty was officially formed. Zhu would appoint members of his family as administrators and local leaders. They were fiercely loyal and his sons soon became feudal Prince's along the River Yangtze. Zhu Yuanzhang was the only Chinese Emperor to have been born a peasant.

His grandfather had served under the Song Dynasty in the Army and Navy. Many think the stories his grandfather told is what inspired him to reform China and return it's former glory.

Even with good intentions he soon dealt with the corruption of the administrators as the system began to replicate former Dynasties. A secret police was formed, called the Embroidered Uniform Guard. They would go onto execute tens of thousands of corrupt officials, dissidents and political enemies.

In his efforts to rebuild a powerful Chinese nation and dynasty Zhu implemented some fantastic policies. Personal slavery was forbidden, large private estates were redistributed, hereditary household titles were issued for societal structure and free movement made illegal.

This saw huge growth and the remnants of former dynasties and their positives re-emerge. However, what started out as the Empire that reclaimed China from the Mongols soon turned into a national cartel.

After the death of Zhu Yuanzhang and his predecessor, the Jianwen Emperor Zhu Yunwen, the culture and trajectory of the Empire changed. The capital was first based in Nanjing but soon moved to Beijing when the third Emperor of the Dynasty – Zu Yongle came to power.

With this came massive Urbanization and the increased complexity of the division of labour. The largest urban centres, Nanjing and Beijing contributed to the growth of private industry, but also presented some of the largest issues.

The Hongwu Empire had built the Dynasty and territories on self sustaining communities, farming communes and agricultural output. Unlike the former Song or Yuan which had supplemented agricultural trade with the merchanting of art, science, culture and even the service sector.

Therefore the city economy and stable urbanisation had to be relearnt, starting with the small-scale industries. The emergence of traders and businesses specializing in paper, silk, cotton and porcelain goods became a new economic foundation. These hubs of trade soon turned into small urban centres with their own microclimate of markets. This model then spread across the country.

With this progress also came the hindrances of xenophobia and common intellectual introspection, a characteristic of the largely popular school of neo-Confucianism.

Even with this disdain for foreign culture it was foreign trade that would ultimately bring stability. Contact and exports to the outside world increase and the economy began to flourish.

Much of this national attitude of disdain for foreigners was directed North (at the Mongols) and not to their main trading partners of Japan. Much like the former Song Dynasty the Ming Empire put huge focus on ocean trade and exploration. In this era Chinese merchants explored the Indian Ocean and even made their way to East Africa.

The dynasty built a strong and complex central government, which unified and controlled the empire on a semi localised scale. It did not share the same synergy and macro vision as previous Dynasties largely due to the Emperors devaluing or eradicating senior officials.

Because of this the emperor's role became more autocratic. Although the Hongwu Emperor abolished the Chancellors position he did continue to use what he called the "Grand Secretariat." This role was given to an expert administrator who managed the immense paperwork of the bureaucracy. It was very much like the role of a modern Prime Minister. His role and sphere of work included memorials, petitions and recommendations to the throne, Imperial edicts in reply, reports of various kinds and tax records.

It was this very level of bureaucracy that would prevent the Ming government from adapting to various changes in society, which soon became one of the core reasons for it's fall from power.

The Yongle Emperor made huge efforts to extend China's influence beyond the nation state. When the Dynasty came to power it self isolated for the sake of recovery, but this shifted almost entirely when it came to trade and exploration. The Dynasty demanded foreign lands send Ambassadors with tributes and vice versa. In addition to this a huge standing army of one million men was formed. Once combined with a monstrous navy, which utilised newly developed four masted ships, the Ming Dynasty became a powerful adversary and world power.

Vietnam was conquered over a twenty year period. The Indian Ocean was dominated by the Ming Navy. The Empire readjusted to an economy more like the Song than the Yuan and domestic life began to thrive once again.

The Grand Canal was expanded and became a stimulus for trade, transport and growth. More than 100,000 tons of iron was produced and utilised every year. Books were once again printed using movable type, and the Imperial palace in Beijing's Forbidden City reached its current state of splendour.

The potential of South China was finally realised in this time. Imported and newly discovered crops were widely cultivated allowing for new cuisines. This in turn boosted the industries producing porcelain and textiles.

The Dynasty would enter an age of relative domestic peace. This lasted until 1449 when Esen Tayisi led the Oirat Mongol invasion of Northern China. It resulted in the capture of the Zhengtong Emperor at Tumu.

From this point on the Ming Dynasty went on the defensive, particularity at the northern frontier. This would lead into the Ming Great Wall being built. The majority of what remains of the Great Wall of China today was either built or repaired by the Ming.

When the Yongle Emperor died the Dynasty became increasingly isolationist. The Navy and Merchant seafaring reduced dramatically, with overseas voyages and expeditions in the Indian Ocean being discontinued entirely.

A maritime prohibition and laws banning Chinese from sailing abroad were enforced. European and other foreign traders that had reached China in this period were rebuked in their requests for trade. Eventually it was the

Portuguese who were first to be physically repelled by the Ming at sea, both in 1521 and again in 1522 at Tuen Mun.

Soon all overseas trade was then made illegal by the state. Wokou piracy soon took a prominent role in society, giving many veterans or desperate individuals a means to survive. Pirates were known to patrol and attack the South East coastline during the rule of the Jiajing Emperor from 1507–1567. This was only contained with major military suppression as the port cities of Guangdong and Fujian were opened.

Soon the Portuguese expanded their Empire and were allowed to settle in Macau in 1557. They would remain there long after the fall of the Ming and worked fairly peacefully with the Dynasty from this point on.

The same cannot be said for the Dutch Empire, who had entered the Chinese seas and met with fierce resistance. After battling with the Ming Navy in the Sino-Dutch conflicts of 1622–1624 they would eventually settle in Taiwan.

The Sino-Dutch conflict continued until the Battle of Liaoluo Bay in 1633. The Dutch were defeated by the Ming loyalist, Koxinga, after the fall of the Ming dynasty. The Ming Dynasty also faced the deadliest earthquake of all time in 1556, during the rule of the Jiajing Emperor. Now known as the Shaanxi earthquake, it killed around 830,000 people.

The Ming dynasty started out as an ally and trade partner to Japan. However, the Dynasties involvement in the Japanese invasions of Korea in 1592–1598 cast a long shadow over a positive relationship. The invading Japanese forces would withdraw from Korea due to the Ming Dynasties support. This led to the restoration of the Joseon dynasty, a traditional ally and tributary state.

The peace and regional hegemony of the conflict had come at a cost, the Ming dynasty was preserved but it's Northerly efforts had taken a huge toll on it's resources. In addition, the Ming's control of Manchuria was in decline, which led the Manchu or Jurchen tribes to break away.

Their Chieftain, Nurhaci and his tribe soon emerged as a powerful, but more importantly unified state. The Ming Dynasties most elite Army was stationed to the Shanhai Pass to guard against the Manchus. Whilst there the Manchu forces conquered Korea, Inner Mongolia and the outskirts of the Great Wall.

Whilst this went on the Ming Dynasty faced even more internal turbulence. Mass scale peasant uprisings rocked the Dynasty and ultimately weakened it enough for an easy takeover by the Manchu's, who would become the Qin and last Imperial Dynasty of China.

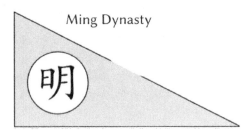

DECLINE OF IMPERIAL CHINA AND THE QING DYNASTY
1644ad – 1912ad

The Qing dynasty was the very last imperial dynasty in China. Having been founded by the Manchus (formerly known as the Jurchen Tribes) the Dynasty would rule the entirety of China proper.

Having taken control of the Ming Dynasty Territory the Qing would double it's size and become the Second Conquest Dynasty to conquer and rule the whole of China.

The Qing Dynasty was declared in 1636ad when the Chieftain King Nurhaci united and then amalgamated all the Jurchen tribes. Part of it's success can be attributed to the Eight Banners System which Nurhaci employed. He is also notable as he formed and spread the new Manchu Language, via written script. Both of these achievements set the foundation for his descendants to conquer the rest of China over 268 years.

After several peasant rebellions within the falling Ming Dynasty, the Manchu military aligned with General Wu Sangui. They took control of Beijing and forced the last Ming Dynasty Emperor, called Emperor Chongzhen to commit suicide. Beijing was then made the capital city of the Qing dynasty and would become a hub for the political and military conflicts in the South. This said conflict with the South would last for decades and lead into the Eastward campaigns.

The Qing were proactive in their fight to expand the Empire and defeated all other powers across China. The entire conquest is estimated to have take as many as 25 million lives.

The culture of the Qing Dynasty was personally influenced by the early Manchu Emperors. They combined the traditions of Central Asia, Historical China and Mongolia with the Legalist and Confucian system of Government.

Policies of the Dynasty were heavily affected by the North Eastern Heritage of the ruling class. As such Han Chinese men were forced to adopt the Manchu queue hairstyle and disregard their traditional hairstyles and clothing. Officials within the Government were also required to wear Manchu-style clothing, to highlight both their heritage and separate them further from the Han People.

Those who wore the Manchu Style clothes of the bannermen dress and Tangzhuang were also treated like landed gentry or nobility. When compared to a traditional Han Chinese citizen they were visually very different, but more importantly they were rewarded with pensions, cloth and land.

This form of ruling class were involved with the creation of the Kangxi Dictionary, by order of the Emperor. They were also most targeted at the time of the Empires Decline.

Early Internal Conflict

There was also substantial conflict within the borders of the Qing Dynasty. Between the years of 1673 and 1681, the Kangxi Emperor would suppress the

Revolt of the Three Feudatories. This had started with three generals in Southern China being denied hereditary rule of large fiefdoms, all of which had been granted by the previous emperor.

Taiwan

Two years later in 1683 the Qing Dynasty invaded Southern Taiwan with the ambition of expanding the Empire. To do so they would be forced to bring about the downfall of the rebel Kingdom of Tungning. The Kingdom of Tungning was founded by the Ming loyalist Koxinga, or Zheng Chenggong in 1662. When the Southern Ming fell and the Qing Dynasty rose the Kingdom of Tungning (Singapore), served as a base for continued Ming resistance.

Russia

The Qing defeated the Tsardom of Russia in the Siege of Albazin from 1685 to 1686. After the Russian surrender they conceded the city and abandoned the Amur River Area. The Treaty of Nerchinsk was signed, which gave the Qing Dynasty ownership of both areas, whilst allowing the Tsardom to continue trade with Beijing.

The Empire was ruled by the Qianlong Emperor at the time and it is widely believed the Dynasty peaked in 1796. By this time the Dynasty encompassed one third of the planets population and had one of the greatest economies in human history.

The British

By the 19th century the Qin Empire was beginning to encounter massive issues. As the Empire grew so did the populations desire for further expansion and self betterment. This manifested as a drive for more territory.

The West, ever cautious of the Chinese Dynasties became more involved through trade and diplomacy. Ultimately this led to some years of prosperity, but the differences in free trade and the free market led to conflict.

The British East India Company pressed for the equal recognition of nations and a less involved approach between the Qing Government and private enterprise.

In retaliation the Qing Dynasty outlawed Opium and grew increasingly hostile to foreign Powers. What would follow is now named the First Opium

War, which took place in 1840 and lasted two years. The British were victorious and this would lead to the Treaty of Nanking in 1842. This declared Hong Kong as a British Territory, where the importation of opium and other goods were allowed.

As trade and connections to the mainland and Qing Dynasty improved so too did the use of Opium. This would undermine many aspects of the Dynasty, especially when more foreign powers saw the benefits of such an agreement. Many other nations would set about to replicate the British-Qing relationship after seeing the rise of Hong Kong and shared creation of wealth.

Late Internal Conflict

The end of the dynasty can start to be seen as the major internal rebellions and power struggles emerged. The Dynasty would ultimately collapse from within, even whilst surviving the above mentioned conflicts.

The first of the internal disputes to weaken the structure of the Qing was called the Taiping Rebellion. It occurred between 1851 and 1864. Uniquely it was the only ever rebellion in China led by a Christian religious movement. Led by the "Heavenly King" Hong Xiuquan it was inspired by the European crusades some 500 years before. The result of the Taiping rebellion would be the establishment of a Taiping Heavenly Kingdom.

The Kingdom engulfed more than one third of China proper for over a decade. The court of the Qing Dynasty would yield to it's previous view on Han Chinese and become more focused on equality. In desperation the Qing rulers would even go onto empower Han officials and allow them to raise local armies.

The first battle's saw Christian fanatics defeat the Qing until the Third Battle of Nanking in 1864. The conflict would turn into one of the largest wars in the 19th century. The death tolls are estimated to be close to the 20 million mark.

With such destruction came years of civil and societal ruin. The Punti–Hakka Clan Wars, Nian Rebellion, Dungan Revolt, and Panthay Rebellion followed the Third Battle of Nanking.

All attempted revolutions were suppressed by the Qing but at an enormous cost. Toward the end of this rebellious era the population had lost faith in the Emperor, Imperial Authority and Dynasty. The Army was disbanded and those who remained in their posts were likely loyal to their local official, not the Dynasty. This led to the emergence of clans and numerous Qing regions being run like independent provinces.

By the time of the Tongzhi Restoration between 1860-1872 the Dynasty appeared to have recovered, the reality is far more complex. The issues of the previous years remained and would never really recover. In light of this, the Dynasty, Government and Manchu royal family established the Self-Strengthening Movement.

This movement consisted of institutional reforms, imported Western factories, communications technology and a small scale military build up.

None of this would achieve the goal of restoring the Dynasty and it's former power but these minor reforms did provide some stability; Until they were capsized by official rivalries, cynicism and disagreements within the Imperial family.

Japan

After the defeat of Yuan Shikai's modernized "Beiyang Fleet" in the First Sino-Japanese War from 1894–1895 the Dynasty would attempt to reform one final time.

The defeat soon became a foundation for a New Army and the famous Hundred Days' Reform in 1898. The attempts were led by the Guangxu Emperor, the Philosopher Kang Youwei and Empress Dowager Cixi. The Empress feared the change would cause bureaucratic opposition and foreign intervention. The Dynasty did premeditate all opposition activity and suppress it successfully until the Boxer rebellion two years later.

The Boxer Rebellion

The summer of 1900 would mark the final twelve years of Imperial China and the Qing Dynasty.

The civil and societal issues caused by the Third Battle of Nanking in 1864 had only grown beneath the surface of major reform. Northern China harboured serious hatred for Christianity and foreign values. Seeing the Qing work with other nations and increase trade and openness an opposition militia movement soon emerged.

Named the Militia United in Righteousness or *Yìhéquán* their goal was to rid China of all foreign influence. They were termed 'the boxers' by the British for their martial arts and fighting capabilities.

The Boxers would go onto murder Chinese Christians, missionaries and many foreigners. As they grew in strength they marched on Beijing where the Qing ordered all foreigners to evacuate, not before many were besieged in the diplomatic and foreign legations quarter.

Soon an eight-nation Alliance was formed and sent the Seymour Expedition. Consisting of Japanese, Russian, British, Italian, German, French, American, and Austrian troops the expeditions goal was to free Beijing, which had turned into a city wide siege.

Soon the Boxer and Qing Armies united after the Alliance attacked the Dagu Forts. The Qing Dynasty ordered the Boxers to join the Imperial Armies and a nation wide war ensued.

After horrific fighting in Tientsin the Alliance formed a second, much larger Gaselee Expedition. This eventually took Beijing and forced the Empress Dowager to evacuate to Xi'an.

Once the Boxer and Qing alliance had been defeated the Boxer Protocol was enacted. Whilst this bought peace the Wars conclusion just marked the start of another era of internal conflict.

The Qing Court worked with foreign powers to increase trade and institute New Policies. The goal of which was to lead administrative and legal reform. The actuality of the events was another uprising led by young officials, military officers, and students.

The Wuchang Uprising

The Wuchang Uprising began on the 10th October 1911 and ended when the The Republic of China was proclaimed on 1st January 1912. It was the end of Chinese dynastic rule which had been in place for well over 2,000 years.

Qing Dynasty

TIMELINE OF MODERNIZING REFORMS

1840-1911: The late Qing Dynasty

1862: Expansion of the treaty port system.

1868: Meiji Restoration in Japan.

1870s: The high point of "statecraft."

1895: Japan defeats China, takes Taiwan.

1898: Emperor's reforms fail, conservatives take over.

1900: Boxer rebellion brings foreign retribution.

TIMELINE OF THE REPUBLIC OF CHINA

1911-1949 The Republic of China.

1912-1916: Presidency of Yuan Shikai.

1916-27: Warlord Era.

1919: The May Fourth demonstration.

1921: Communist Party founded.

1927-37: Guomindang unifies part of China; capital at Nanjing.

1927: Communists defeated, retreat to the countryside.

1931: Japanese take Manchuria.

1935-36: The Long March.

1937: Japanese invade North China.

1945: US atom bombs bring Japanese surrender.

1945-49 Guomindang-Communist Civil War.

1949: Guomindang defeated, retreats to Taiwan.

TIMELINE OF HIGH SOCIALISM

1949: People's Republic founded.

1947-52: Land reform.

1954-56: Agriculture collectivized.

1956: Industry socialized.

1957: Anti-Rightist campaign.

1958: Great Leap Forward and People's Communes.

1959-61: Famine.

1962: Retreat from communal to collective production.

1966-69: Great Proletarian Cultural Revolution.

1966-76: The "Cultural Revolution Decade."

1969-78: Youth to the countryside.

1972: Nixon visits Beijing.

1976: Mao Zedong dies.

1978: Official reform policy announced.

TIMELINE OF REFORM AND THE MODERN NATION

1979-82: Dismantling of collective agricultural production.

1979: Beginning of the Birth Planning Program

1984: New constitution allows some freedom of religious practice.

1985: Urban private enterprise allowed.

Late 1980s: collapse of restrictions on migration to cities.

1989: Student movement, culminating in Tian'anmen massacre.

1993: China's Olympic bid fails.

1994: Recentralization of finances.

1990s: Rise of urban consumer society.

1990s: Nationalism replaces revolution as national goal.

1997-2003: Regime headed by General Secretary Jiang Zemin.

1998: Major floods bring turn toward environmental protection.

2001: China's Olympic bid succeeds.

2002-2012: Regime headed by General Secretary Hu Jintao.

2008: Tibetan uprisings, earthquake, Olympics.

2009: Uyghur uprisings.

2012- Regime headed by General Secretary Xi Jinping.

HISTORICAL MYSTERIES

The Ancient Silk Road and Great Wall

Few other world monuments have quite as much mystery, history and legend surrounding them as the ancient silk road and great wall. The silk road itself has been reinvigorated with the belt and road initiative, but the routes which lasted a thousand plus years beforehand certainly have some stories and mysteries.... To read them go to page – 225.

Gansu's Romans

There are white Chinese people and Chinese nationals in China toward the North. These are provinces that were once Russian and taken by China between the 1950's and 1980's. Outside of this European features are rare and recent to the biological mix of the nation.

However, the more secluded regions of Liquan and Gansu Caucasian features can be seen amongst perfectly integrated communities and locals. The understanding of these people is they are the descendants of a captured Roman Legion from the year 36bc.

The city of Xixia and the Tangut People's

In 1227, the Mongols committed one of history's first recorded genocides against China's northwestern Xixia Empire. They city of Xixia was practically flattened leaving no real understanding of the people, their culture or any potential sites. The language and scriptures of these people are still to be translated and understood.

The Haunting of the Forbidden City

This mystery is intertwined with legend, folklore and even some modern allegations. Reports across the cities lifespan have hinted at serious paranormal activities. Claimed sightings of concubine ghosts, large rat like creatures and the spirits of former Emperors have been made from with in the walls of the Forbidden City and based on it's past, if ever there was a likely place this is it.

Longyou Caves
The Longyou Caves emit mystery in it's purest form, not from their visual appearance over the waters on a misty day, but the precision of their design. Despite being over 2000 years old and forgotten about until their rediscovery in 1992, the uniformity of the patterns measure and perfect 60 degree angle parallel chiselling make for a fascinating mystery indeed.

The Ice Age
The end of the Ming dynasty was bought about a short term ice age, which consisted of famines, freak snowstorms and other disasters over a thirty year time frame.

Kanas Monster
There have been sightings of a 15-meter-long creature in Xinjiang's Lake Kanas. China's largest fish, the paddlefish can reach up to 3m in length but is very likely extinct, with the last sighting being in 2003.

The Nameless Lake of many death's
One of Peking University's most scenic spots is also suspected to be the site where murders and mass suicide took place in the Cultural revolution.

The Witches
Whilst we know the Celtic tribes travelled the Silk Road and even settled across central Asia and China, a particularly pagan mystery has been unearthed. Mummies wearing the tall pointed hats of druids have been unearthed in Xinjiang's Tarim Basin. Dating and textile evidence suggest connections to Celtic druids but the mystery and verdict of their magic, witchcraft or make belief is still out.

Submerged City
Whilst not a mystery and actually quite well known about today the Ancient city of Shicheng may even be the best-preserved city in China. It was flooded and completely submerged during the construction of a dam in 1959. The mystery lies not in the history but the hundreds of ghost sightings and claims of haunting.

Yingkou

During an enormous storm in 1938 there were several accounts of an enormous serpent or dragon which derailed a train and sank three boats. The skeleton of this creature was reported as found but soon lost in the war.

Xi'an Pyramids

The 400 pyramids in Shaanxi are shrouded with mystery, their exact age and purpose remain unknown despite their enormous size.

Zombies in Chengdu

In 1995 several bodies were involved in a particularly mysterious disappearance from an ancient tomb. They were never found and reportedly roamed the streets of Chengdu at night for years.

The Unknowns of the Qin Tomb

The discovery and further exploration of Qin Shi Huang's terracotta army, copper-clad tomb and deeper structures have yet to be unopened. Once technology, archaeology and preservation methods have advanced the rest of the system will be explored. Speculation as to what knowledge, treasure and mystery the tomb hold range from a scalemodel of China with "rivers of mercury" to many of the long thought missing manuscripts showcasing the real history of pre-Qin China.

Xu-fu's disappearance

Qin Shi Huang, who is widely believed to be the first real Chinese Emperor was terrified of death. He built the infamous and spectacular tomb with a whole Terra-cotta army and countless other spectacles.

His fear soon turned to desperation and he sought a route to become immortal. He surrounded himself with magicians, shamans, guru's and other spiritual leaders toward his later years. They claimed he could extend his life span with a special potion, so he commanded Xu Fu, a man who told the emperor he knew where to find the elixir of life to find it.

Xu Fu stated that the magical elixir could be found on the islands in the Yellow Sea. This island's inhabitants were both immortal and the protectors of the potion. In 219bc Xu went on an expedition to find the elixir, with him he brought 3,000 virgins who were pure enough to access the elixir. On his return (without the potion) he claimed sea monsters prevented the envoy from reaching the islands. The Emperor Qin sent Xu Fu back to find the elixir, this time with a unit of archers. Xu Fu never returned, but is rumoured to have landed in Japan.

The Stick Case
On May 30, 1615, the peasant called Zhang Chai managed to sneak into the Forbidden City. He would go onto attack a Eunuch with a stick and attempt to break into the palace where the Emperor Wanli's son lived. He was apprehended by a larger group of eunuchs. Initially the court deemed Zhang as a loner and insane. It was not until he sustained torture and maintained his story of a larger conspiracy that he was taken seriously.

He claimed to be working with a larger group of eunuchs who had helped him into the Forbidden City. His role was indeed to kill the emperor's son, Zhu Changluo by order of the eunuchs Pang Bao and Liu Cheng, whom he identified. Zhang was executed and the identified Eunuchs tortured, only to die of their injuries later on.

Zhu Changluo would die under mysterious circumstances five years later, after he succeeded his father as Emperor Taichang.

History of Chinese Civilisations Origins
The Sanxingdui relics are the last remnants of a now untraceable Sichuan Kingdom from 5,000 years ago. They mystery about them is the speculation. If more remnants and evidence is unearthed it could lead to a very different understanding of how the Chinese civilisation originated, and bring severe questioning to the yellow river theory.

CHINESE
THOUGHT

//

''Laws control a lesser person; right conduct controls a greater one.''

思想

THOUGHT

The greatest difference between East and West is how we think. Even in the interconnected and globalised world of today this is still the case. Western and Eastern, specifically Chinese and European/American thought is significantly different, both in terms of methodology, psyche and the general view on life.

This chapter focuses not on the differences between how we think but what causes it.

FOLKLORISTICS

Early thought is developed from the stories we tell our children. Their morality, spirit and later life ethos is very much defined by these tales, myths and legends.

In the West the story will tend to follow a dramatic cycle, where the storyline goes from peace and stability to some form of problem, trouble and hardship to a conclusion. Typically by the time of the stories end the protagonist will have overcome the issue.

Eastern and Asian Folklore tend to follow a different pattern. The examples listed below will show a more diverse and inconclusive story, with several morals, triggers for further thought and much more symbolism, metaphors and allegories.

The fours Great Folk Tales of China are;

- ✗ Butterfly Lovers - Liang Shanbo and Zhu Yingtai

- ✗ Tale of the White Snake

- ✗ Lady Meng Jiang

- ✗ The Cowherd and the Weaver Girl

BUTTERFLY LOVERS

There was a lady called Zhu Yingtai. She was born into a wealthy family and the ninth child. At this time in Shangyu, Zheijiang, the Eastern Jin Dynasty where they lived, ladies were discouraged from becoming scholars and academics. Zhu eventually persuaded her father to let her attend classes in the disguise of a man. Ultimately she would journey to Hangzhou as a scholar.

Along her journey she met a scholar called Liang Shanbo, who was from Kuaji, now present day Shanbo. They felt an immediate affinity for one another and soon affirmed their feelings through an oath of fraternity. After gathering soil as incense they unified under the pavilion of a wooden bridge.

For the next three years they studied together, Zhu still in her disguise as a man and Liang failed to recognize her feminine attributes and habits. After being engrossed in books and studies Zhu received a letter from her father telling her she must return home. She packed her items and said a sad goodbye to Liang. On leaving she revealed her true identity to the headmasters wife, pleading with her to give Liang a jade pendant as a betrothal gift.

She new in her heart that she wanted to be with Liang for eternity and he accompanied Zhu for 18 miles on the journey home. On this journey home Liang believed he was simply accompanying his sworn brother and not a women home.

Zhu tried to reveal her identity through the comparison of Mandarin ducks, a traditional symbol of lovers. Her hints failed and they were soon forced to say their goodbyes at the Changting Pavilion.

Just prior to this Zhu came up with the idea to at least see Liang again. She told Liang she would introduce and partner him with her sister, who was the perfect match. He agreed and several months later comes he came to their home to make his proposal.

On his visit he quickly discovers that Zhu is a women and the story of a sister was just a ploy. They take their vows and officially devote themselves to one another.

This time of joy and happiness was short lived. Zhu's parents had already pre-arranged for her to marry a wealthy merchant. His name was Ma Wencai and the wedding was to go ahead. On hearing this, Liang, who was by now a country magistrate died of heartbreak whilst working in his office.

When it came to the day of the wedding heavy winds prevented the ceremony from going ahead. Zhu could not meet Ma as the wind was so strong the procession could not pass the grave of Liang, which was on route. As she went to pay her respects she begged for the grave top open. With an enormous clap of thunder it did.

Before anybody could stop her she threw herself into the grave to be with her one true love. No more than a moment later two butterflies emerged and flew away.

TALE OF THE WHITE SNAKE

There were once eight immortals. One of them went by the name Lu Dongbin. One day he decided to disguise himself as a vendor on the broken bridge, close to the West Lake of Hangzhou.

Whist in his disguise Lu Dongbin sold a young boy called Xu some Tangyuan, when in fact these were pills of immortality. For three whole days the young boy could not eat a thing. He returned to the vendor on the bridge and asked ''why?''

Lu Dongbin did not answer but laughed, instead of answering Lu picked up the young boy and violently flipped him upside down over the bridge. Xu vomited straight into the Tangyuan lake.

Beneath them was a White Snake Spirit, who ate the vomit and the pills as they fell into the water. The snake spirit, having practised the Taoist magical Arts was granted 500 years of magical power. Observing this from afar was another spirit in the form of a Terrapin. He did not manage to consume any of the pills and became very jealous. Some time later at the same lake a peasant caught a green snake, with the intention of killing and butchering it to sell its gall.

On realising this the White Snake transformed itself into a women and bought the green snake from the peasant. Having been saved by the white snake the green snake was grateful, loyal and regarded it's saviour as a sister.

18 years of peace would pass until the two now friendly snakes snakes transformed into two young women via the magical power granted by the beans.

The white snake took the name Bai Suzhen and the Green snake Xiaoqing. Having been intertwined by fate they would go onto meet a much older Xu at the same broken bridge.

Xu and Bai Suzhen eventually fell in love and got married. They moved to Zhenjiang and opened a Medicine shop. In all this time the spirit in the form of a terrapin had been building his strength. He could now take human form and transformed into a Buddhist Monk called Fahai.

Being jealous of their happiness he began to work on a scheme to force the married couple apart. In his new human form the Terrapin Spirit, disguised as the monk Fahai met with Xu at the Duanwu Festival. He told him that it would be good to get his wife a drink and try the realgar wine, the most common alcohol of the festival.

Xu soon bought his wife the drink, which she sipped. As she swallowed the wine her true form as a snake began to take shape. Seeing this Xu died of shock.

Bai Suzhen and Xiaoqing would travel to find the magical herb on Mount Emei and restore Xu's life the next day. They found the herb and with a great deal of effort brought Xu back to life. Xu's love for Bai remained true even after knowing about her true form.

Hearing this Fahai is outraged and begins his next attempt to destroy their love. Fahai then captured Xu and imprisoned him at the Jinshan Temple. Soon Bai Suzhen and Xiaoqing go onto fight with Fahai to try and save Xu. Bai uses all of her power to flood the temple, which not only failed to rescue Xu, but killed many innocent people. Her powers had decreased since she was already pregnant with Xu's child.

Xu eventually managed to escape from the temple by himself and reunite with his pregnant wife in Hangzhou. It is here where she gave birth to their son named Xu Menjiao.

After a several years of peace Fahai managed to track them down and defeat Bai Suzhen. He imprisoned her in the Leifing Pagoda, leaving Xiaoqing no other option but to flee and make a vow of vengeance.

Xu Mengjiao would take the Imperial Examinations to bring glory to his parents and soon returned home. Over 20 years had passed and Xiaoqing, the green snake had been practising to defeat Fahai once and fore all. On entering Jinshan Temple Fahai is defeated and fled to hide in the belly of a crab. In doing so he turned the stomach orange. Soon after, Bai Suzhen is reunited with her husband, son and friend.

LADY MENG JIANG

The story of Lady Meng Jiang has survived centuries as it remains relatable to many people today. There are many variations but the core story is that Lady Meng Jiangs husband was forced into service as a labourer.

The Imperial Guards sent him to help construct the great wall and took him whilst Lady Meng was preoccupied. For some time after his departure she would hear nothing from her husband. Fearing he would be cold as winter approached she bought him his warmest clothes.

On arriving at the Great Wall she discovered her husband had been killed, like so many others in it's construction efforts. One hearing the news she cried so forcefully that a part of the Great Wall collapsed to reveal her husbands bones. She soon died of sadness and her tomb was built into the wall. Located in the Shandong Province it has been reconstructed over the past two thousand years as it continues to fall.

THE COWHERD AND THE WEAVER GIRL

One of the most prominent love stories of all time 'The Cowherd and the weaver girl' is really quite beautiful. The weaver girl is not a human but a star. The cowherd is not a farmer but also a star.

Their love for one another was forbidden and they were banished to opposite ends of the heavenly river, which is also known as the milky way. Once a year on the seventh day, of the seventh lunar year a flock of magpies form a celestial bridge, which allows the lovers to reunite for one day.

The variations of this story are numerous and it also forms as a foundation which many other tales are built on. The tale of the

Cowherd and the Weaver girl is more than 2600 years old and has spread throughout the Asian continent.

PHILOSOPHY IN CHINA

Mainstream philosophies are the prominent influencer of a persons mentality. In China religious, spiritualist and philosophical thought have merged. The leading and historical streams are;

x Taoism

x Buddhism

x Confucianism

x Legalism

x Mohism

TAOISM

Taoism is sometimes known as Daoism and credited to Lao Tzu. It has become both a philosophy and religion through the lessons and principles it promotes. The most accepted of these is doing what is natural and "going with the flow."

There is also the principle of the Tao or Dao, a cosmic force which flows through everything. It also has an effect of binding and releasing them. In the West a large part of this understanding can be related to the thought of a spirit or nature of someone/something.

The Core Beliefs of Taoism: Taoist thought focuses on – vitality, genuineness, longevity, health, immortality, detachment, refinement (emptiness), spontaneity, transformation and omni-potentiality. The idea of 'wu wei' is prevalent, it means to have a perfect equilibrium with the Tao through non-action and natural action.

BUDDHISM

Buddha means "enlightened." Buddhism means the path to enlightenment via the course of attaining and utilizing morality, meditation and wisdom.

In China and many other Asian nations Buddhism is a religion. It's off shoots and sects operate as collectives and religious movements alongside the main stream thought and belief. Outside of China and Asia Buddhism is often classed as a way of life, a spiritual movement, a philosophy or even a personal ethos. For example, many people are Christian in religious belief but also practice Buddhism.

The Core Beliefs of Buddhism are:
An encouragement to avoid self-indulgence and the act on the teachings of the Buddha. Buddhism is aimed solely at the liberation of sentient beings from suffering. The core principles of Buddhism can be found in the 'The Three Universal Truths', 'The Four Noble Truths' and 'The Noble Eightfold Path.'

The Four Noble Truths are the essence of Buddha's teachings.
x) They are the truth of suffering,
x) The truth of the cause of suffering,
x) The truth of the end of suffering,
x) The truth of the path that leads to the end of suffering.

The main principles to Buddhism are;
x) Refrain from taking life / Not killing any living being.
x) Refrain from taking what is not given / Not stealing from anyone.

x) Refrain from the misuse of the senses / Not having too much sensual pleasure.

x) Refrain from wrong speech / Not lying or gossiping about other people.

x) Refrain from intoxicants that cloud the mind.

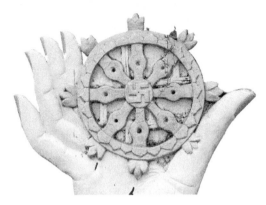

CONFUCIANISM

Confucianism is characterized by it's influence on China, it's social values, it's institutions and the overall historical impact of it. As such it is more of an ethical philosophy rather than a religion, but still massively important in modern China.

The Confucian belief was based and is built on ancient religions. Therefore the spiritual elements are well founded and indeed more than just a way of thinking in many respects. Today those who practice Confucianism are focused more on society, the state and the real world, not the afterlife or spirit.

Core beliefs of Confucianism and Confucius:

The worldly concern of Confucianism or Confucian belief is that human beings are fundamentally good, teachable, improvable, and perfectible through personal and communal endeavour.

Confucian thought focuses on the cultivation of virtue in a morally organised world via self-cultivation and self-creation.

Main Pillars of Confucianism:

x) Xin - Honesty and Trustworthiness.

x) Chung - Loyalty to the state, etc.

x) Li - includes ritual, propriety, etiquette, etc.

x) Hsiao - love within the family, love of parents for their children, and love of children for their parents.

LEGALISM

Historically Legalist's advocated for government by a system of laws. This led to the traditional view of them being devoid of character and quite boring. In reality they bought order to a society when most of the world were still living in tribes. Via the strict enforcement of punishments and rewards for specific behaviors, Chinese society began to thrive. The common man reflected the Legalist philosophy throughout Imperial China, rather than resort to aggression.

The movement powered the direction of all human activity. It forced society toward the goal of increasing the power of the ruler and the state, whilst protecting people equally.

Legalism speculates that humans are naturally inclined to wrongdoing. Therefore the authority of laws and the state were absolutely required for human welfare, societal balance and progress. This school of thought is opposed to Confucianism and the belief in the inherent goodness of human nature.

MOHISM

'The School of Mo'

Mohist's and those who believe in Mohism advocate a philosophy of impartial caring. It is not so much that they discard care, but care equally for all individuals on the same scale, regardless of their actual proximity or relationship them.

Mohism is one of the oldest philosophies in China that still influences the modern nation. Dating back to 470 BC to 391 BC the thought was progressed by academic scholars who followed the philosopher Mozi. It encompassed attributes of other Chinese philosophies, but with a deeper link to emotion, science and reason.

Mohism as a spiritual, religious and philosophical movement formed the backbone of the Social theory for Communist China. Today it is not so much practised in ceremonies or openly spoken about but within pro-communist circles it is well known; But as a main system of thought it is slowly going extinct. As the nation continues to evolve and become more commercialized this philosophy continues to decline in popularity.

POLITICAL THOUGHT

Current political thought in China is uncharted territory. No
Government to date has blended Capitalism and Communism like
modern China and the average opinion correlates to this. Most people
understand the authority of the state and do not question it by
exploring alternative political theories. This unique approach to policy
has worked, China is functioning on an evolving political thought
which continues to be influenced by;

MAOISM

Chairman Mao's Political and Military Philosophy is still prevalent in
modern China. The policies of the modern nation are still based on the
Communist and Socialist ethos he implemented. Even with modern
restructuring and innovation the core of Policy is still Maoist
Communism. When it comes to Maoism it is easy to separate it from
Marxist and Leninist Political Theory. The core difference is in the
power given to the poorest members of Society. In Maoism the
peasantry are the most important aspect to society, not the
proletariat.

- Difference -

x) The proletariat is the class of labourers and working class, the ones
that swap their time, life and health for a wage.

x) The Peasantry have nothing.

The reason behind this difference in Marxist/Leninist Communism
and Maoism is the capacity for revolution. It is the poorest of the
poor, (the Peasant Class of people) who are most likely to revolt and
commit to it with their lives.

In the pre-Mao era the families and communities of the middle to upper class were gaining distance from the poorest individuals. This increased as Western investment strategies allowed wealth to be created by capital and money alone. Soon the divide was near enough impossible to close.

Mao adapted Communism to counter the wealth gap, disengage foreign influence and restore China. The Maoist political thought is widely accepted to be a positive, even in light of the accidental atrocities of the regime and era.

As it happens the comparisons to this era and today are fundamental in understanding modern China. Maoism took hold of China until the end of the cultural revolution. What followed was a more intricate and flexible form of Communism, which can be linked to Dengism.

DENGISM

Dengism is the political ideology from the 1970's to 1980's, employed by China's then leader Deng Xiaoping. It does not reject Maoism, Marxism or Leninism but adapted the theology of the time to fit current China and the global conditions. This modified political thought allowed for growth and the movement of an older era of China to re-emerge. Capitalism was not entirely shunned and the blend of Communist values and Capitalist Practice built the China we see today.

It is this style of China which harbours economic growth and is almost like a different model of Communism. In many ways it has resulted in a national structure more similar to a national socialist framework than true Communism. Many people will say Dengism marks the end of state Communism, others will say it refined and fixed the political movement into something that actually works.

Dengism and it's associated Communism cannot be put on the spectrum of 'ultra left, left, centrist or even centre right' because it takes elements of them all. It is the only form of Communism that has survived the era and allowed for unscalable development of modern China.

OVERSEAS STUDENTS

Every year just under one million Chinese Nationals leave China to study overseas. This figure has steadily increased by ten percent every eighteen months for the last decade. This exodus, or migration in search of education has benefited the Chinese economy, industry, sciences and professional sectors, but it's real value is in the cultural exchange.

These overseas students typically return to mainland China having built relationships with foreigners, westerners and added value to the city or school they studied with. This of course influences their own perception, psyche and Chinese Thought as whole. The extent of this fairly large segment of society bringing back alternative and typically non-Chinese philosophy is yet to be seen, but very interesting.

Westernisation, Commercialism and Communism
Understanding the Modern Chinese Psyche

China has done something that no other communist or former socialist nation has. It has managed to build a modern capitalist state with a communist foundation and character.
In doing so the public have benefited from a strong state and core, with a semi free and state monitored market. This physical and national trait is reflected in the modern Chinese psyche.
Westernisation of China is being prevented via state regulation. The State is all powerful and will likely remain in control of the commercial and communist movement, therefore continuing to balance the positives of the two and progress the nation further.

As the next generations come to purchasing power the Communist tendencies seem to fade, but this is far from true. Whilst consumerism and the demand for materialism increase the philosophy of Communism prevails. It was not just inherited from past generations but to this day the belief in Communism is inspired.

Unlike other nations the State and Government showcase internal power. Every Chinese national over the age of thirty can see the

81

change of the nation. In other words it is possible to see what the nation has achieved with this blend of capitalistic-communism.

In seeing this most people will adopt a similar personal philosophy. There is also a growing Nationalist movement which mirrors the popular loyalist psyche of the Imperial Dynasties, which was always followed by growth.

The Culture and Politics of China are partial influencers of this modern psyche, which seems to transcend class or education level. It is the examples in society as whole and the family community which are the main contributors to this understandable collective psyche.

CHINESE
POLITICS

/ / /

"China is a sleeping giant. Let her sleep, for when she wakes she will move the world."

- Napoleon Bonaparte

POLITICS

China has awoken.

If you don't recognise this, or even that China is the new World power then it's time too. Even with it's global and internal issues the country continues to rise economically and influentially. As the rest of the developing world partners with China it's place is secured even further.

Modern China, like it's evolution of Communism has reshaped domestic policy and global affairs. Trade links, supporting businesses and political influence are tools of modern China. It is through enterprise that the nation has gone from factory of the world to arguably the most influential soft power in human existence.

It is essential to understand Chinese Politics wherever you live.

Chinese Politics, likes all politics is a non-linear, multi faced beast. Add in the variables of a mighty population of one billion plus people, cities in the tens of millions, a strong and growing sense of nationalism, and we can begin to get a very basic understanding of Chinese political stability.

A volcanic eruption is the most suitable allegory for modern China and it's politics. Before a volcano erupts it causes earthquakes, tremors and a deep rumble. This rumble can be felt for decades before the main eruption event.

Post eruption one of three scenarios can happen.
1. The world can either be destroyed in a wave of ash, dirt and destruction;
2. The initial destruction can create new land mass or fill once arid areas with fertility, minerals and opportunity;
3. The Volcano can return to it's constant state of rumbling and pre-eruption.

In this volcanic scenario China is the physical Volcano and the rest of the world is the surrounding land. The precursors to eruption have been seen and now we must all await the main event. The revolution, economic reform and massive development took place in the last century and now it's show time.

Where there was once nothing in China, Central and South East Asia, Africa, South America, Europe and North America there is now Chinese business, infrastructure, technology and influence - at all levels.

You can see this right now, just look to the closest piece of technology as it was almost definitely manufactured in the city of Shenzhen or China. Your local city will have a Commercial Bank of China, the state owned Private

Enterprise which is also the biggest bank in the world. But this interconnection and link to China goes far beyond manufacturing and banking. Roads, railways, mines, political lobbies and national partnerships all over the planet are being led and fostered by China.

Whether this volcano calms or rises to a world changing delivery of magma, lava, steam, business, political efforts and global affairs will be seen in the next few decades.

How this change happened and more precisely, how China has managed such a feat (in it's pre-eruption days and in so short a time frame) is entailed in the following pages.

THE CHINESE GOVERNMENT

''A Socialist consultative democracy'' is the technical term for the Chinese system of Government. What this means is the republic is divided into the State, Executive, Legislative, Judiciary and then multiple parties.

The 'President' is the Head of State, 'The Premier' or 'President of the Executive' (Yuan) is Head of the Government and the Executive is comprised of all the non elected civil servants.

All very similar to the Western framework based on the ancient Greek model of Democracy so far, the differences come later. The Judiciary of China are also a separate and an independent body from the executive and legislative branches.

The Power of the Party within China is the real difference between China and the rest of the world. China has had one prominent Party since the modern nation materialised, therefore spending zero time dealing with the bureaucracy and inefficiency of other political systems. The Chinese Communist Party, with a membership of 90 Million people has had consistent power since it's inception.

Being the last of the great Communist states Chinese communism has evolved to avoid extinction like the Soviet Union. It is this current day model of Communism that seems to work and the nation claims that Communism has not yet been achieved, but it is still being worked towards.

The modern Political framework takes the core Marxist and Leninist principles and has diluted them over time. In doing so they have catered for a controlled but free economy. This has created a freer market than most true capitalist states.

It would also be proper to define what is meant by China. The nation and country has been inward looking and cyclical for thousands of years. However modern China is still cyclical but now looks outward with a new realm and increasing disputes. The modern China we know is as old as the CCP or Communist Party of China, since they took power. Everything before the revolution is 'old China' and closer to ancient History.

The Chinese Constitution establishes the Republic of China as the mainland nation with Six Special Municipalities (The six major Taiwanese cities, portions of the Fujian province and several smaller islands in the South China Sea.) There are also thirteen other external counties and three more cities counted as China.

The Constitution stating this was formed in 1947 prior to the Communist revolution, but amended 44 years later. It is also worth noting that the Communist party is stated within the constitution as being outside the reaches of the law. Which until recently has allowed numerous cases of corruption and back hand dealing to take place.

The characteristic of untouchable leaders is central to the 'old China' as well. Since the Mongol Empire, Great Dynasties and even the Golden Age of the Middle Kingdom, this regions leaders have always been placed above the law by the mandate from heaven.

After several nation changing Judicial interpretations these amendments in 1991 highlighted a flaw that the old constitution. By readdressing what was defined as China, this adaptation to the constitution helped form and eventually materialise a new vision of China and it's future.

PRESIDENCY AND POLITICAL STRUCTURE

The President of China has authority over the five administrative branches of Government. The Executive, The Legislative, Control, Judicial, and Examination are the five branches or the Yuan. The first national government of the Chinese Republic was established on the 1st January 1912, in Nanjing, with Sun Yat-sen as the provisional President.

Provincial delegates were sent to confirm the authority of the national government, and they later formed the first Chinese parliament. The power of this national government was both limited and short-lived, with generals controlling all of central and northern China. Military conquests, instability and a lack of understanding led to turmoil. In short this earliest form of Government led to the abdication of the Qing Dynasty and marked the end of the dynastic era.

It was during these years that a man named Yuan Shikai rose to power. He was a supporter of the Qing dynasty and despite his best efforts the Monarchy failed, even so his royalist tendencies and loyalty remained. Yuan was an all rounder with skill, experience and educated in bureaucracy, economics, the judiciary, the military and teaching. With this unique skillset and his genuine ability to drive China back to stability he certainly made history, but failed to achieve his goal.

History really has tarnished Yuan negatively, mostly due to his attempt of becoming the new King or 'Hongxian Emperor,' after becoming the first President. Yuan also led the republic of China through some of it's earliest trials. The Wuchang uprising, abdication of the thousand year old dynasties, Japans 21 demands and the introduction of globalisation and democracy were all challenges in which he faced. Increasingly many Historians argue he may have amended and fixed the constitution to better himself, but also did so for the sake of the nation.

POLITICAL EXPANSIONISM

China has taken over the markets, industry and much of the world through partnership, friendship, business and diplomacy. Saying this, it would be wrong to continue without mentioning one of the rare times China has not used soft power to gain new territory or influence.

Taipei, the capital of Taiwan has long had a history of wanting independence from China, if not sole control. As it stands right now, Taiwan has independence of it's island state, albeit an informal and not entirely free from influence model.

If Taiwan were to formalise then Mainland China has made it sufficiently clear over the years that it would or could lead to war. As such, the nation has continued in a perpetual state of uncertainty, which is starting to be seen in homeland frustrations; With clever politics from the Taiwanese Supreme

Court and National Assembly the situation is unlikely to change anytime soon.

But if war does arise, however unlikely, then China will exert the power of it's now formidable defence forces.

THE HONG KONG PROTESTS
2019/2020

The core issue of this event in China's recent history is a surge for control. China was not the core violator in the riots and nor was it the cause, this was the Hong Kong Government and the Fugitive Offenders Amendment Bill. The introduced bill, (if it is to be enacted in the future) would allow for the legal extradition of wanted persons, criminals and fugitives, to namely mainland China and Taiwan.

Whilst the Bill is at present suspended and the extradition of 'undesirables' sounding like a positive on the surface, it is in fact in the murky waters of backhand dealing and corrupt officials, or so the Hong Kongers say. In addition to this many have also argued there would be an opportunity for the bill to be used for political gain.

Even worse than this, it could lead to the undermining of the more open, pro free speech and liberal environment of Hong Kong. Some even argue if the bill is passed then it will act as a gateway to mainland Chinese law taking precedence and Hong Kong losing it's autonomy over the long term.

The Bill was suspended but the riots have continued in mid 2020, whilst only being halted en masse due to the global Coronavirus pandemic.

A FREE TIBET?

The arguments between those wanting an independent Tibet and the Tibetan Autonomous region as part of China likely predate the most accurate historical documents available. As it stands Tibet is a part of China and with those that support this saying it has been this way for 800 years, since the Yuan Dynasty.

It has therefore become a Chinese state and inseparable. In addition to this the country of Tibet, (if it is real) would be recognised by other nation states, which it has not. In the true sense of the word Tibet is not a Nation, it has been without the formal title for some time and despite the unique culture, language, religion and system of governing it remains very much a part of China.

Saying this, it is not since the 1950's when the China as we recognize it, took a more active role in the area. It started with a military presence and of course cases of rogue units raiding and trading, but in short the Chinese forces agenda was just to reaffirm the state as a part of greater China.

Since this time Tibetans have fought for independence and it is only now where we can see the scale of both arguments. China's overpowering culture, military, infrastructure and vision is depleting the individual character, image and way of life in Tibet, which leads to its own problems.

The relatively new involvement of the United Nations bringing human rights claims against China in Tibet is also escalating the situation. From an international law perspective Tibet remains an independent state under illegal occupation, but of course this can and has been argued about for generations.

SINO-INDIAN BORDER DISPUTES

The 2017 Doklam Military standoff is the closest we as a planet have come to a War involving the only nations with a billion plus nationals.

Of all the causes and reasons for it starting it turns out to be over a piece of isolated, uninhabited wasteland. For the sake of face or ego this chunk of 'borderland' has been in dispute between the Chinese and Indians for several hundred years. With road building, development and bored soldiers the area has turned into a bit of a boiling pot. With increasingly frequent skirmishes and in some cases soldiers fighting to the death the area is unlikely to play down in the short term. Even with India and China agreeing to 'expeditious disengagement' and a more relaxed stance the events and tensions continue to fluctuate.

FOREIGN POLICY

Chinese Foreign Policy is undergoing a revolution of sorts, and as far as the outsider can see it is one of global ambitions. In truth there are only a select few at the highest levels of Industry and Government who really know the end goal, but evidently it is to further secure China as the new world power.

There is of course massive suspicion towards the extent of China's diplomatic and international relations goals. Reliant or competitive nations will legitimize their malpractice when it comes to their efforts in securing China as a partner, but for the most part up until mid 2020 this has been mutually beneficial from an economic and industrial level.

China's diplomacy flows through industry, so when they build relations they also build business. Which is where nefarious nations can cipher funds or act unfavourably. China has gained influence and partnerships with favourable conditions in their foreign efforts, and this is the goal echoed by the diplomatic leaders.

The nations official foreign relations statement is that it "unswervingly pursues an independent foreign policy of peace. The fundamental goals of this policy are to preserve China's independence, sovereignty and territorial integrity, create a favourable international environment for China's reform and opening up and modernization of construction, and to maintain world peace and propel common development."

This is a beautiful agenda (by foreign policy standards) but there have been some aspects to the contracts which bring some concern. Whilst good business practice for conditions to be enforced if terms or payments are nor kept, it is unusually to see nation states handing over national assets as collateral or reparations. This has happened mostly in China's African partner nations, but also Sri Lanka and South East Asia. Chinese Foreign Policy only extends to the point of nations that acknowledge Taiwan as an independent state.

This indirect strong arming has been a cause for concern and even lead to criticism or outright defiance and conflict. Some would argue this mentality toward foreign policy looks like the early stages of every nationalist, colonial, empirical or some would argue extremist approach of history. The cold, hard reality is we will only know of China's true intentions by the time it is too late.

INVOLVEMENT WITH INTERNATIONAL ORGANISATIONS

Over the last 50 years China has become a member of nearly all international organisations. Today it holds positions of power within all of them. The United Nations is where China has been most active, as a powerful member of the UN Security Council the advances in Non-Proliferation of Nuclear Weapons, Global Policing and Security, Global Governance and Peacekeeping operations have been areas of active involvement.

China, whilst being far from the EU has immense power through direct and indirect bureaucracy. It will likely never come to light but the truth of the Covid Warnings, whether it was in fact three clear warnings, some propaganda or even an EU softening of the pandemics extent in favour of public opinion in the early days are all topics of huge discussion, or conspiracy theory.

The Association of South-east Asian Nations is also an area in which China has made some recent changes, both in action and behaviour. Being the most powerful nation in this region and group, the sway has once again turned in it's favour and regional stability is in China's hands.

The yearly talks to promote regional security, both in the ASEAN states (Brunei, Cambodia, Burma, Indonesia, Laos, Malaysia, Philippines, Singapore, Thailand and Vietnam) and the ASEAN Plus Three, (India, New Zealand and Australia) have allowed for the spirit of China, it's hard infrastructure, trade and industry to bring about development all over.

CONTINUED DISPUTES

The reason for a heavy handed approach in the following disputes is partly due to China's involvement in the above partnerships, and partly down to the increased necessity for peace.

It is also wise to note that the younger generation of Chinese are coming into positions of power in the ruling party, most of which have foreign educations. Whilst territorial disputes are clearly one of the main aspects to tarnish the modern nations reputation, this new approach of waiting and winning in a reserved manner, through commerce and culture is playing in it's favour.

RAILROADS
BELT AND ROAD

As the US- China Trade War took serious casualties in both nations, China set about to expand the Belt and Road Initiative. Which is perhaps the greatest diplomatic and trading asset to ever exist. Based on the ancient silk road, which connected East and West for four hundred continuous years over a thousand years ago it has been equally successful.

It is also unique as China has been active in the construction of almost all rail roads since their beginning in Great Britain. The Belt and Road Initiative has mirrored the historical trade route as a mode of expanding territories, ownership and influence. The areas, resources and business connected to the road all feed back to the economy of mainland China.

These multinational trade agreements are how China has developed informal relationships with Europe, Greater Asia and Africa. Each nation involved in the massive contracts will offer the best of their assets, resources or business in return for access and partnership.
This all leads Governmental oversight and allowing the public officials of China and the partner nation to meet and build relations. The belt and road initiative is almost certainly derived or inspired by the Chinese leaders, who in post cold war China decided to change tactics to maintain presence in the global arena. It is in fact near genius to use almost covert, soft and submissive tactics on such a mass scale to increase global influence, with close business support.

Seeing the fall of the Soviets and Communism become redundant in Europe must have been a huge driving force for China. As the world entered this new era of Super Pacts, Alliances and the age of America, China did not commit effort, commerce, loyalty or money to any of these areas.

Instead the nation maintained focus on its internal functioning and next to nothing else, which of course paved the way for Modern China's success. As the nation began to balance out and run in isolation, combined with the evolution of Chinese communism a huge foundation for overseas trade and relations was built.

Even today, with China being a member nation to many Alliances and Pacts the focus is still very much internal and on China alone. By becoming involved and privy to the agendas and conversations in these organisations it allowed the learning and growth curve to be taken home and used to even greater effect.

The Belt and Road began in 2013 and has resulted in infrastructure agreements and development in 70 plus countries. The officials who are vocal on the strategy say the purpose is "To construct a unified large market and make full use of both international and domestic markets, through cultural exchange and integration, to enhance mutual understanding and trust of member nations, ending up in an innovative pattern with capital inflows, talent pool, and technology database."

The Belt refers to land transportation and the roads to Ocean based transport. The target completion date and basic interconnection of the entire planet is 2049, also the hundredth birthday of China.

DIPLOMACY

Diplomacy in China is cultivated to the point of being artistic. Until recent times we have seen guile take precedent over ferocity, but times are changing. In light of the nations defence of the pandemic outbreak, and the events leading up to it, the personality and character of Chinese diplomats has been revealed.

For the most part the average diplomat of any random nation takes a career in this field for its diversity, travel, perks, level of engagement and overall quality of career. The Chinese equivalent is highly educated and a firm believer in the ruling party and its goals. Increasingly we see younger individuals take up senior positions and with this young blood the identity and ambitions of the new china become more active.

The Chinese Diplomats making a difference also receive a celebrity like status with their efforts being known to their thousands of colleagues and millions of Party Members. This interconnection within the actual Diplomatic efforts, combined with social media and instantaneous global publicity make the returns for a job well done, or recognition massively superior to any other Government role.

This is fuelling an effort for superior results. The ambitious diplomats who know their success and failure will be known to an enormous amount of people will of course be working to better the nations, which might be interpreted as aggressive foreign policy.

The famous Qin Gang, China's Foreign Ministry Spokesmen announced in 2007 the 'Eight point philosophy' on Chinas diplomacy.

93

1. China will not seek hegemony. China is still a developing country and has no resources to seek hegemony. Even if China becomes a developed country, it will not seek hegemony.

2. China will not play power politics and will not interfere with other countries' internal affairs. China will not impose its own ideology on other countries.

3. China maintains all countries, big or small, should be treated equally and respect each other. All affairs should be consulted and resolved by all countries on the basis of equal participation. No country should bully others on the basis of strength.

4. China will make judgment on each case in international affairs, each matter on the merit of the matter itself and it will not have double standards. China will not have two policies: one for itself and one for others. China believes that it cannot do unto others what they do not wish others do unto them.

5. China advocates that all countries handle their relations on the basis of the United Nations Charter and norms governing international relations. China advocates stepping up international cooperation and is against unilateral politics. China should not undermine the dignity and the authority of the U.N. China should not impose and set its own wishes above the U.N. Charter, international law and norms.

6. China advocates peaceful negotiation and consultation so as to resolve its international disputes. China does not resort to force, or threat of force, in resolving international disputes. China maintains a reasonable national military build-up to defend its own sovereignty and territorial integrity. It is not made to expand, nor does it seek invasion or aggression.

7. China is firmly opposed to terrorism and the proliferation of weapons of mass destruction. China is a responsible member of the international community, and as for international treaties, China abides by all them in a faithful way. China never plays by a double standard, selecting and discarding treaties it does not need.

8. China respects the diversity of the civilization and the whole world. China advocates different cultures make exchanges, learn from each other, and complement one another with their own strengths. China is opposed to clashes and confrontations between civilizations, and China does not link any particular ethnic group or religion with terrorism.

THE POWER OF CHINESE OFFICIALS

There is an opinion held by many foreigners and even Chinese nationals that many Chinese Officials are corrupt. It goes without saying where there is a man or women with power they will at some point be tempted to a moment of weakness or moral corruption. Times that position and person by a scale of three million Government Officials and these cases will be a considerable number.

Many local and regional Officials in China in the 80's, 90's and 2000's had a flexible understanding of legal and unofficial but the current administration has flattened this. The modern party has reduced corruption enormously and the odd case of an Official being corrupt at a high level in China today is broadcasted.

The corruption of Chinese officials tend to follow the pattern of a 'single mistake' or 'one off moment of weakness.' Not years of taking bribes and abusing of power, which might have been the case in the past.

The nation, government and party is so vast that regulation and assessment of an officials character is difficult, but becoming easier.

The lower and mid level Officials are of course the hardest to monitor, if they are acting illegally and in the rural or inland regions. Even with such a vast scale the Officials with real power and influence are cracking down on those who are acting illegally, with the full force of the nation. So much so that the effectiveness of the crackdown is exceeding the conviction rates (Statistically) than much smaller and far more corrupt nations, showing the system is working.

The modern China as we all know is still a young nation. In young nations it is proven that nationalism is fiercer and more prominent and things like corruption more prevalent.

Saying this the sense of identity and serving your country is the desire of many Chinese nationals, especially the youth of today, which gives hope for the future.

Between 2013 and 2016 a million Chinese officials were punished for corruption. This drive to eradicate corruption by the President ranged from low ranking officials to senior party leadership, the media and the public-private sector. As this young nationalistic segment of society joins the ranks it will allow corruption to continue to decrease as well.

The only thing that can't be changed in the mid to short term is the conditions of making easy bribes across mainland China. With such close ties between private industry, the public Sector and public servants, bribery and corruption is inevitable and near enough impossible to stop in some regions. On a case by case basis, it does beg the average layman like myself to question - If there is a million plus cases of corruption, does the average party member or official have too much leeway?

The answer is of course the scale, the difficulty with oversight and the nefarious nature of some minority or niche individuals in the Government. This scary understanding, without being too presumptuous, is a question Senior Chinese Government Officials are asking themselves with the current efforts.

MAIN LEGAL DIFFERENCES BETWEEN CHINA AND THE WEST

Sino Law is essentially Civil Law with a Socialist twist.
Whilst defined as a socialist legal system it bares immense similarities to Europe and the United States systems. The modern system is not like the historical Socialist Republic's and their systems in the slightest. The Constitution is the highest law in China and with clever involvement in International Organisations there is little international influence, oversight or precedence.

The Law on Legislation only allows the National People's Congress and it's standing committee to make Laws. This is the countries top legislature and is enforced by the Supreme Court of China. The Judicial System is not clear and simple for a foreigner in particular. Due to the age of the nation and Organic Law of the Peoples Courts 1980, it really has enabled a lot of the ingrained tradition, historical dimensions and structure of the Greek, Roman, English and American systems to be amalgamated into China's four court system.

The Supreme People's Court is the highest court and deals with the largest, most important and final cases of the nation. When lower courts are involved with cases acting across provinces or territories it is these Supreme People's Court Judges who preside over the hearings, either in Beijing or in one of the circuit court seats in the relevant province.

This court also supervises the lower courts to see the accurate administering of justice whether they be "local" or "special." Local People's Courts are similar to County or Magistrates Court in the West. They are first to handle criminal and civil cases and make up the three remaining levels of the Chinese Court system.

Local People's courts are broken down as such:
- ✗ High Peoples Courts deal at at the level of the provinces, autonomous regions, and special municipalities.
- ✗ Intermediate People's Courts deal at the level of prefectures, autonomous prefectures, and municipalities.
- ✗ Basic People's Courts deal at the level of autonomous counties, towns, and municipal districts.
- ✗ Courts of Special Jurisdiction are made up by Military, Rail and Transport, Maritime, Internet, Intellectual Property and Financial Courts. All of which, except military come under the jurisdiction of the High Court.

JUDGES

Becoming a Judge in China is also very clear, potential Judges must pass the National Judicial examination and this is public knowledge. In much of Europe there is still some mystery around how one can become a judge.

POLICING

Policing in China is probably the most dynamic public sector service of them all. It varies in consistency and strategy probably more than any other nation on earth. If in the rural or inland regions Policing will be typical of that region, more traditional and reliant on old school Policing tactics.

Areas like the North West will have a massive police presence for the security risks and very active Policing of everything. The developed cities of Shanghai and Bejing will have a broad range of Policing styles and Units, with some looking futuristic and practising advanced counter terrorism procedures right down to a normal traffic police officer in a luminescent vest.

The main thing to bare in mind when dealing with the Police in China is to be aware of their powers and the differences. The Police do not have nearly as many restrictions on their powers as in the West. They do not need a warrant to search your property or persons. It is best to follow instructions and comply with all Police as the nature of the authority is quick to quell opposition.

Procedure, (assuming your not involved with serious crime) is also very different. If the civil wrong can be dealt with before entering the formal legal system it is typical to do so. This agreement will be made with both parties taken by the police for a cup of tea. They will then negotiate and advocate the best outcome.

THE NATIONAL CONGRESS AND MODERN COMMUNIST PARTY

The National Congress is the parties most powerful and highest body. It was formed to undergo six main responsibilities:

- ✗ Electing the central committee.
- ✗ Electing the Central Commission for Discipline Inspection.
- ✗ Examining the report of the outgoing Central Committee.
- ✗ Examining the report of the outgoing Central Commission for Discipline Inspection.
- ✗ Discussing and enacting party policies.
- ✗ Revising the Party's constitution.

The reality is Officials don't really discuss pressing issues at length in the national congress, this is reserved for top party leaders, in the preparation stage and for National Congress.

If an issue needs a solution between periods of gathering the Congress, (like supervising anti corruption, ethics and disciplinary action) it is the responsibility of the central committee and central commission for discipline inspection. These then elect smaller bodies to carry out the foot work.

The interconnection between public sector organisations and the main Government can also be seen in the case of the central committee. The Secretariat is the highest body in the Central Committee and responsible for reporting to the rest of the Central Committee and supervising sub departments. The Central Committee is also the very top of the line when it comes to military decision making and appointing or dismissing top military officers.

It is this organisations role to co-ordinate security strategies across numerous departments, including intelligence, the military, foreign affairs and the policing aspects. They do so to evolve activities and cope with growing challenges to stability at home and abroad.

It is the General Secretary of the Central Committee who has the real power. Unlike other parts of the party and government who utilise collective leadership, the Central Committee is reliant on the General Secretary, who also takes the title of Chairman.

Other areas controlled by the Central Committee include communications, protocol, and setting agendas for meetings. These are achieved by the four main departments, the Organization Department, the Publicity Department, the International Department and the United Work Front department.

The Central Committee is also in control of the Central Policy Research Office, the Central Party School, the Party History Research Centre, The Compilation and Translation Bureau, The Newspaper 'People's daily,' the magazines 'Seeking truth from the facts' and 'Study Times,' the Central Finance Office and many 'Central Leading Groups' like the Hong Kong and Macau office and the Taiwan Office.

At a sub division level the Communist Party of China extended it's command to all government institutions and social and economic organisations.

The current system is modelled off of the Soviet system called Nomenklatura where each sub committee and department operates on it's own level. It has the power to recruit, train, monitor, appoint and relocate officials.

Party committees exist based off Geography and demand. They can be located at province, city and county level, whilst influencing local policy by incorporating local leaders into the activities.

Uniquely the Party Secretary at each level is senior to the leader of the government, with the CPC standing committee being the key source of power. We can clearly see the Central Committee is the heart of Chinese Government. It pumps the actions that fuel the nation at almost every level, which is far from what the West is used to with numerous parties, councils, departments, states and a changes in Government near enough every election.

LOBBYING

Lobbying in China is not what we in the West understand it to be. Political Lobbying in China is normalised into the Government system with both official and unofficial avenues proving effective. The majority of internal Chinese Lobbyists are industry focused, rather than charitable or non profit based. The pedigree political lobbying of China takes place outside of the nations borders, with special interest groups who act on behalf of the Government.

Lobbyists and Special Interest groups of China and Taiwan act on behalf and often in conjunction with one another. Most commonly they aim to better Sino-American, Sino-European, Sino-everyone relations and the bigger picture foreign policy.

The State and Private sector of China are interconnected on a scale unseen like anywhere else in the worlds free markets. To give some scale, the 50 largest companies in the world consist of 10 state run Chinese enterprise.

For the most part this has aided China's massive growth in such a short time. In addition to assisting foreign policy and economic growth these companies have acted as tools to spread positive Chinese opinion and culture. Which is a fantastic strategy for spreading positive Chinese national opinion and lobbying for the best interests of the nation.

CHINA AS A CYCLICAL POWER

Global perception and the popularity of China is truly diverse. In the last decade it has never been so high until the events of the Coronavirus Pandemic. Chinese Nationals naturally hold their mother country with great esteem and are more often than not patriotic. Statistically this transcends the ratio game of those working for the public sector or those being assisted by it.

It is the support of the middle class, those on middle to comfortable salaries that maintain the favour of the state. The other nations with the highest ratings of respect and positive view on China include Pakistan, Tanzania, Bangladesh, Malaysia, Kenya, Thailand, Senegal, Nigeria, Venezuela and Indonesia.

These nations favour China for one of three reasons.

1. The Infrastructure and trade agreements China is bringing to their nations, resulting in improved quality of life and infrastructure.
2. In the cases of Pakistan and Bangladesh a powerful and stronger China is better than a more powerful and stronger India, and due to China inherently winning the Asian power struggle this increases public thought.
3. History, similarities and association.

The nations with some of the lowest opinions of China include Japan, Vietnam, Turkey, Italy, Germany, India, Poland, Jordan, The US and Colombia. Some of these nations have been subject to contract law and had to forfeit assets or industry, some have lost once global manufacturing industries to the Chinese models and some have an outright religious, psychological or cultural opposition to the nation.

Throughout history China has risen to power and greatness, peaked and then entered long periods of instability, relative chaos and a lack of authority. It has followed this pattern since the times of the Dynasties and it is now, under the banner of the modern nation that the whole world is watching to see if this cyclical curse is now extinct.

MOVEMENT OF PEOPLE

China has focused on the movement of people more than any other nation throughout world history. For some reason even the earliest accounts have a focus on the clear and detailed logs of human movement. This can be seen in the documentations left by scholars writing about bride stealing in the Liao and Song, the Yuan dynasty promotion of inward migration and even today where the largest migrations in History are taking place.

The flow of people into and out of China has been turbulent throughout history, with whole era's banning free movement and others promoting the increase of global foot traffic. Uniquely, the characteristic of moving to find or undergo work has been the exception and continued, as is the case even today.

Those travelling the silk road for trade or as part of the massive public workforce which built the great wall were always exempt from strict travel permissions.

Today, those Chinese nationals leaving the nation typically do so for business purposes, or of course holidays. The vast majority of modern movement and foot traffic takes place inside China's borders. This focus and future of human movement within China is going to be a colossal aspect to global balance. As the nation continues to urbanise and liberalise the population trends will dictate global resource demand.

The focus of the past has been inward migration into the cities, supported by Government Policy. This saw five of the largest ever human movements take place, the first and largest being the flow of people into the city of Shenzhen. This high tech metropolis with an unofficial population of near 20 million people was nothing more than a fishing village in 1970's. After being designated a special economic zone in the 80's it has grown at a trajectory of a 100 percent every year. In 1950 the population was reported at just under 50,000 people and by the year 2000 it was well over 6,000,000.

The rate of growth has not slowed and Shenzhen is but one example of the scale of human movement in China. As Government policy changes so too will the flow of people into the cities. In fact the goals set by the Authorities are now like a reverse migration scheme, employing the same policy of creating special zones outside of the cities.

With 60 percent of China living in cities in 2020 there has been a huge emphasis placed on the push back to the country side. Over the next century the grandchildren of the nations workforce will begin to move back home, away from the megacities and into the rural farming towns and mountain hamlets. With this next mass migration those involved will bring wealth, business and much needed stimulation to impoverished areas. Undoubtedly they will produce interesting results and new world firsts as well.

CHINESE
INDUSTRY

////

''In every Crisis there is opportunity.'' - Chinese Proverb.

行业

INDUSTRY

China started out as the nation we know today in 1949.
From 1950's to the late 1990's it became the hardware factory of the world.
By the year 1990 it had become the most advanced manufacturing centre for all goods, a hub for the service and design sectors and the fastest growing society in world history. By 2010 the middle class was the same size as the whole of America and demand for resources put national focus on the primary and resource sector. By 2020 Chinese banks, software services and investment overseas connected the strong domestic economy with the global markets.

Between 2020 and 2030 China sets the goal to import over $22 trillion worth of goods, showing the full cycle from being a low import and high export nation to the worlds largest importer. Major development projects will continue thus developing the rural regions as well. Since the nations beginning the State has played a significant role in Chinese Industry. The Government is actively involved with industry, not just in policy and practice but in ownership, collaboration and assistance.

TRADE WARNINGS AND WAR

The US-China trade war had been a long time coming and both sides are equally biased as to the 'why?' President Trump, when elected in 2018 implemented tariffs and trade barriers. His argument being that China employed unfair trade practices and were actively stealing American business and ideas.

These forbidden practices in America have been taking place in China since the manufacturing era of the 90's, and only grown with time. When China officially became the factory of the world in the late 1990's to early 2000's the trade deficit increased, which then forced the transfer of American Tech to China on an unparalleled level. Some argue it was voluntary, some would say strategic and many claim large scale cases of intellectual property theft.

The trade war taking place is built on this foundation of 'cause' which resulted in the tariffs by both the US and China. To be perfectly honest, the scenario we see today is much like a game of checkers. It is without a clear winner like the game, but also boring, pointless and only leads to short term wins.

THE TECH SECTOR

The Tech Sector, (specifically the manufacture of the entire planets hardware) is what powered China's rise to the top of the new world order. The last 40 years is where we can actually see this take place, with the creation of special economic zones, top down planning, the influx of rural based families to the rapidly expanding new cities and truly enormous amount of cheap labour.

This all led into one of the last great ages of industrialisation. It is likely that manufacturing will never see levels like China in the late 1990's again. High tech and robotics have taken over and uniquely this has had an effect the world has never seen before.

As the bubble of labourer based manufacture reduced in influence, it neither peaked or exploded, unlike historical eras of rapid development which taper off to an era of unemployment.

It is this foundation of a new tech sector where the masses of factory workers have shifted peacefully into different avenues and work that is incredible. Most have risen to form the new middle class of China, which in turn carry an enormous cash flow and stimulate further growth.

This is perhaps the most fundamental change to the economic transformation of China as a nation. Where local economies flourished so to does culture, the service sector, and perhaps most importantly the average persons own ambition.

When you take a subsistence farmer and pay them properly in a manufacturing job (when compared to what they are used too) they have families, and a sense of faith and desire for their children to live a better life.

This generational transition and evolution of those working in the tech sector has led to;

x Drastic changes to societal structure, showcasing that millions of factory workers can indeed rise into the middle class.

x The tech sector is actually changing the infrastructure and channelling the whole nation into a new age and area.

x The natural overflow of success into other sectors and industries.

THE GREAT CHINESE FIREWALL

What is it?
The Chinese Government have a series of technological and legislative procedures in place to limit the internet freedom in China.

What is the purpose?
Whilst it is argued that the Firewall is a fair form of domestic regulation and a truly remarkable technological feat is is enforced to;
1. Blocks access to certain foreign websites and information sources.
2. It slows down cross border traffic.
3. It forces foreign companies to adapt their sites and services to the nations regulations.

4. To nurture domestic companies and create an enclosed operating area.

By doing all this the Government can accurately analyse data, establish a full access internet dialogue with the users, and foster home grown business.

Does it work?
Since it's inception in 2006 and completion of phase two in 2008 the firewall has worked, until 2018 and 2019. It is in this time where the world wide web has been accessed with smartphones and free use VPN's. The Great Firewall is operated by the Cyberspace Administration of China, which needless to say is advanced to the point of being scary, and aware of the Firewalls shortcomings. This will be the body that determines the future of the firewall and whether it continues in this next era of rapid technological development.

INTELLECTUAL PROPERTY THEFT
SHANZHAI GOODS

Since the 1980's and technological explosion China has been in the picture and holding up the mass markets. The biggest tech companies of the 1990s soon made their way to China and built their hardware. This initial move soon led to more high tech developments until we see cities like Shenzhen match and even surpass the most high tech capitals of the world.

The reasons for this change is obvious, cheap labour, massive efficiency, speed of production, availability of materials, logistics and relative ease of transport all made for an excellent climate. The influx of major companies and their manufacturing also triggered startups at a scale that has never before been seen.
These startups, whether they are legal, unregistered, illegal or in a grey area are the main proponents to the intellectual property theft allegations.

There are many claims of Chinese business stealing other nations business ideas or products. Outside of legitimate corporate espionage and theft the opinion below is most accurate.
In China, during the tech high point of the mid 1990's saw numerous senior engineers leave the industry leaders with the knowledge and expertise to start their own businesses.
How much they took with them from the original companies is open to debate, but the fundamental understanding of this whole scenario within China is opensource.

Copyright and Patenting is practically non existent in China, therefore opensource has become the norm. Idea's are not owned and the freedom to pursue a near identical product drives progression for the sake of market positioning.
There are millions of small 'mom and pop' enterprises in China as well. Within the tech sector they may be making replica goods and selling for cheaper prices but this is understood and accepted.
The real issue with this topic is a niche movement (again still on a massive scale) who wear the term Shanzhai with pride.
Shanzhai means mountain village or mountain stronghold. A place where bandits operated away from the control of the authorities. It

now refers to an individual or group that counterfeit consumer goods, particularly electronics and technology - under the same trademark as the original.

Many leading Shanzai brands were formed by these former engineers, scientists, production managers and tech minds of the original companies. After becoming unsatisfied with their pay, life or without a real belief in the original company, they then took (stole) the wireframes, blueprints and technical details and started garage operations. These have since grown into billion dollar enterprises across China and the rest of the world and are Shanzhai.
It can be argued that rather than destroying the fair and open market they simply operate on a different model, or as it was back when they started out the 'Wild West' era of China's development, it was very much an "anything goes" attitude and commercial foundation.

SHENZHEN

It is not possible to speak of the Chinese Tech Sector and avoid the topic of Shenzhen. A city of more than 20 million people and widely called the Silicon Valley of China is undeniably the tech capital of the nation and perhaps even the word. It's an incredible place.

It's name (Shen Zhen) means deep drain, as the area was rice paddies and a drainage basin no more than fifty years ago. The city as we know it was the first of China's special economic zones. The city is home to the headquarters of Huawei, Tencent, China Merchants Bank, ZTE, OnePlus, Global Financial Centres Index, Shenzhen Airlines, JXD, Hytera, Vanke, CIMC, SF Express, Nepstar, Ping An Bank, Hasee, DJI, BYD and many more companies and business.

It is more than the combination of several thousands startups, the Shenzhen Stock Exchange, it's port and the government incentives for all this growth. Nobody can really put a name to the feeling Shenzhen gives you, between the mass markets, unique little beaches and culture there is something indescribable here. What we can describe is how the construction and infrastructure has mirrored this growth trajectory. With now more high rise buildings and sky scrapers than any other city Shenzhen is the metropolis of the future.

Whether these once old and slow paced fishing villages can turn into something replicating a Utopia or Dystopia is dependant on the tech sector. The economy and growth will continue, but the variables determining whether the city will be a polluted, dirty and painful place to live or something truly beautiful is in the balance. Tech, engineering, environmental surplus projects, conservation and sustainability need to be further incorporated into the metropolis or things will go ugly very quickly.

SHENZHEN AND HONG KONG

The rivalry and struggle for power between these two cities transcends Technology. Both cities favour growth and both want to be the image of a new China. It is here where the rivalry begins. Hong Kong is tradition, history, refined culture and old school ambition. It is a former colony, trading post and holds several millennia of culture and history. It has been the first point of call for all those who enter China by sea and remembered fondly across the world.

Shenzhen is likely younger than some of you reading this. It is the pinnacle of modern Chinese development and liberal, innovative and a mainland Chinese exception. Being located next to one another, the cities are slowly morphing into one. This is leading to turmoil as both city states are suspicious of one another, more so the Hong Kong residents being sceptical and fearful of a mainland Chinese takeover. With this threat of a true Communist takeover and reduced liberty we see the foundation of the Hong Kong riots. Both cities aspire to be the pinnacle of modern China, Hong Kong with it's open policy to the rest of the world, a sturdy service sector and overall better quality of life, Shenzhen with it's unparalleled drive, ambition and centralised national control.

TECH SECTOR CONTROVERSIES

There is no point listing the positives of the Chinese Tech sector as they would fill this whole book. Instead, to get an all round understanding of the sector it is best to focus on the controversies. Huawei is a big name, both in China and around the world. They offer technology at the same level as many other leading brands, but typically at cheaper prices. It is this success that has bought light to several controversies and questionable practices. Overlooking the personal controversies linked to the company it is only worth mentioning the larger organisational happenings.

State Support of Huawei is common knowledge, the only question left is to what extent? Despite the company being so large there is little to no public information on the ownership and breakdown of shares owned, and by whom?

The reasons for such a collaboration in the eyes of many is that Huawei is a tool for Chinese Government surveillance and an asset in the cybersphere. It is argued Hauwei is used for cyberespionage, cyberwarfare and cybersecurity. Huawei was also a core component in the US-China trade war, the company formed a foundation that allowed alleged and wilful violations of US Sanctions against Iran. Huawei has also been accused of hardcore intellectual property theft from several companies. Cisco, T-Mobile, Nortel all claim theft from Huawei and T-Mobile US caught an industrial spy taking photographs of a robotic stress tester for mobiles and trying to steal a core proponent (A specialist fingertip.) Huawei Senior leaders all claim that the US is biased and targeting Huawei for the sake of eliminating a threat to US business.

TENCENT

Internet in China and Tencent go hand in hand. If the largest websites of the world all merged together their combined services would form a similar service as to what Tencent offers China. The services offered by Tencent include but are not limited too – entertainment, artificial intelligence, video games (it is the worlds largest video game company) one of the largest venture capital firms, social networks, music, web portals, e-commerce sites, internet services, mobile games, apps, online games, payment systems, smartphones, instant messenger and literally hundreds of other products and services. Each one of the categories Tencent operates in it becomes the market leader. The company has passed the US$500b point in record breaking time and continues to grow at a trajectory which could see it as the worlds largest company.

The controversies associated to it, even with it being on such a huge scale are not proportionate to its rivals. In 2019 a number of international security agencies confirmed Tencent was used as a surveillance and censorship mechanism, which is understandable. The issue was this activity began to creep into the mainstream devices and services offered to other nations. It is this intensity and the fact that they may be observing users beyond the Chinese Homeland which has led to controversy.

INFRASTRUCTURE

Infrastructure in China is as much a part of the landscape as the natural world. It is a product of the culture, society, wealth and shared ambition of many Chinese. When much of humanity were still living in tribes, with the equivalent infrastructure of a mud hut or cave, the Chinese had conquered hydroponics, roofing, roads, carving, moulding, sculpting, painting, timber-work, carpentry and building. This combined with Asian, Eurasian and European exchanges the role of infrastructure became fundamental to China and it's business interests.

This infrastructure quickly evolved to form the foundation of the 'Golden Age' of Dynasties in China, going from Sweeping roofs to castles and forts. Perhaps the most iconic symbol of China is a piece of infrastructure - The Great Wall.

Modern Chinese Infrastructure is perhaps the most unspoken aspect effecting the global environment, perhaps matched only with India's infrastructure in terms of global anonymity to sheer disruption of conditions. The by-products, side effects and direct results of Infrastructure, development and influence on the whole planets future, be it from a political or environmental perspective is wholly overlooked. Infrastructure within China, or involving China across the planet can be divided into three main studies;

1. Infrastructure as an economic and political tool to secure China's interests.
2. The changing face of Chinese cities, towns, villages and regions.
3. The future of Chinese infrastructure.

Infrastructure in China is a multi faceted tool, used not just for the development of the home territories but also other nations. It is infrastructural ability that has made the belt and road initiative a reality, which in turn has led to China's interconnection with the world and trillions of dollars in trade agreements. Infrastructure has now made China the new owner of the African continent.

By building roads, railways, sewage systems and other infrastructure in return for resource rights China have developed these nations, fuelled there own economy and expanded their sphere of operations and control. This also goes on via a different scale throughout Asia, Europe and The Americas, across all industry types. The first nation in Europe to join the belt and road initiative was Italy which reignited the historical significance of Sino-Italian relations.

Infrastructure on the Mind
The Infrastructure of China is also moulding the nation. The physical environment not only effects the health of those living there, but also their mind and behaviour. Infrastructure conditions the mind and all sense of psychological balance, the further it gets from nature the more corrupt the mind becomes. We see this evolve in China as the nation's cities went from low level, ornate urban style villages to hard communist architecture to the now 'free for all' of high rises.
The culture and the mentality of such unnatural development has responded. Civil engineering from a perspective of harmonic living is second to profit margins.

With enormous amounts of traffic the infrastructure for electronic vehicles is also on the increase. Which is one of the first steps to restoring a balance between growth and sustainability. More pressing to Greater Chinese Infrastructure systems is the topic of smart cities. Surveillance is incorporated into the core features of the Chinese urban environment. When you go through a modern Chinese city you are unknowingly involved in the 'big bother' concept.
The ten most effective surveillance cities in the world are all located in mainland China. Thanks to the 'Sharp Eyes Initiative' the State is actively watching everyone.

This behavioural monitoring is more open than other nations as there is some level of public interaction with the data. If you are being monitored and your behaviour is deemed untrustworthy or illegal, the data in many locations is made public on advertising boards. Other citizens can then shame, apprehend or at least be aware of the individual.

This all came around from a method of assessing ones driving abilities, credit score and other daily interactions. This original idea has morphed into massive, multi platformed surveillance.

Combined with the monitoring of devices and technology on a macro scale the infrastructure and smart cities are all gearing up to procuring a truly safe and secure state, or quite the reverse, it all depends on who you ask.

In addition to this, there is the fantastic concept of reward and punishment for the good and the bad. Assuming the idea is not corrupted those who add value to society or behave will receive rewards (like reduced bus ticket prices) and those that cause problems can be sorted out quickly.

All of this development does lead to a better world, if one core aspect is introduced and nefarious reasoning is indeed not behind it.

The one core aspect to bettering Chinese Infrastructure is the incorporation and amalgamation of eco projects, pollution balance schemes, clean energy production and developing areas of surplus natural beauty or conservation in the urban settings. If this is achieved China will secure it's place as the most formidable nation when it comes to humanities infrastructure.

INFRASTRUCTURE TALKING POINTS

Within China there are at least 11 life size and replica European towns, cities and landmarks. They can be found at;
- Hallstatt in Guangdong.
- Paris in Tianducheng.
- Holland Village in Pudong.
- Sweden Town in Luodian.
- Thames Town.
- Anting German Town.
- Breeza Citta di Pujiang.

113

- Florence in Tianjin.
- London's Tower Bridge in Suzhou
- Château de Maisons-Laffitte in Beijing
- Pont Alexandre III in Tianjin (Beian Bridge)

GHOST CITIES

Within China there are large uninhabited or very minimally populated cities, developed to cater for the next generations growth. Being isolated but close to overpopulated cities many of these developments lay empty in wait. Some have resulted in developers going bankrupt and development stopping completely.

This unique trait in China's infrastructure shows the core difference in the Construction sector and urban development of China and the rest of the world.

Rather than having thousands of independent developers all scramble to build one tower block huge areas are allotted for large companies to build upon.

This combined with the rapid capabilities of developers, (who utilise prefab more often than traditional methods) allows for buildings and infrastructure to go up left, right and centre. A few of the most famous Ghost Cities that are only just starting to change after a decade of laying still are:
- Chenggong District
- Ordos City, Kangbashi Area
- Nanhui New City
- Yujiapu Financial District
- Yingkou
- Lanzhou New Area

See Page 239 for Architectural Developments

FASHION

Style and Fashion within modern China is changing just as quickly as everything else. Traditionally fashion and the fashion industry within China have fallen into the below dress-codes.

Day to Day

x Unpretentious, simple and conservative are the buzzwords of the everyday clothes. Women should avoid showing their backs, thighs, or chest with minimal jewellery.

Business
x For business attire the expectations are similar to that of traditional industry. Smart, clean, suits or dresses are the go to. However, like the industry standard across the planet the national expectations of China and the rules around fashion are changing.

Difference
The fashion markets of the West and China do have one major variance. Everyday Chinese brands make an effort to preserve cultural style. There is a partial movement which aim to avoid the total internationalism that comes with modern high fashion, which is refreshing. As the high streets around the world begin to enter their last days due to online retail the age of the Super Mall in only just starting in China. This is because of infrastructure and population numbers. There is a hidden element of modern society in China fuelling Fashion and the in person experience and stores which provide it. This sect of society is the young, professional and semi wealthy ladies.

CHINATOWNS AND CHINESE EXPATS
There are 100 million Chinese nationals living outside of mainland China. That is more overseas nationals than the actual nationals of Germany, Great Britain, Canada, Australia, France, Spain, Turkey, Saudi Arabia and most other developed nations. Whilst most have integrated into the societies they now live in, many decide to add value and hold some ties to China through the Chinatown's.

Found in every major city on the planet these Chinatown's have been the soft expansion of Chinese global dominance for centuries. Through migrants fortifying the links to mainland China the infrastructure and Chinese influence has got a base and foundation in every major city on the planet. In this sense the Chinatown has acted much like the US militaries use of bases across the world. These microcosms of mini Americas around the world benefit the local

economy and fortify American interests. Chinatown's do the exact
same thing.

CHINESE SOCIETY

V

"Talk does not cook rice."

MODERN CULTURE, SOCIETY AND ECONOMY

If we take away globalisation, politics and business it is the culture of modern China that has allowed it to thrive as a nation state. Deng Xiaoping said 'Socialism does not mean shared poverty' and this is what moulded the current society of China. A socialist State with a semi free market and the ability for those willing to work hard enough for a better life can actually achieve it.

This started in the eighties and now second and third generation wealth is relatively commonplace. Whether it is the form of a communist society Mao envisioned we will never know, but it is a system that many would now say is working.

A clear way to look at the society is similar to how we can grade animals. A pedigree is a pure breed, it has been refined through years and generations of breeding. A Mongrel is bred by selecting two different types of parents and letting natural selection do the rest. Both mongrels and pedigrees can work, be beautiful, coexist and live a happy life.

It is therefore clear to put American society in the bracket of a pedigree capitalist economy and China in the Mongrel form. They, much like litters of animals need each other or inbreeding will occur. China's economy, through natural selection has become a highly effective mongrel breed. What is most unique, is that the Pedigree Capitalist society of America and the Mongrel economy of China need each other to survive, just like animal species to prevent in breeding.

The culture of Modern China is less formed now by history and more so by the Government. In China the private sector is still answerable to the government. In America, capitalism is the government as they are so intertwined.

Many see that this State control of the society in China as a positive and in many ways it is. The Father figure of the nation provides security, an order and protection from the many negatives we now see in the West and completely liberal societies. China is socialist but there is no freeloading like the economies and governments of Europe who get taken advantage of. Within China there is a set limit to liberal attitudes, everyone is more or less accepted (with a few exceptions) but the society would shun those looking to increase their own status by finding loopholes.

China avoided that swing of neo-ultra liberalism entirely, while in the West we start to see the negative implications of allowing 'self identifiers' and other extreme liberal movements rise as influencers. By maintaining societies connection and constant awareness of the Government it has allowed for culture to really take prominence once again. So much so that many see modern China restoring the legacy of the golden era of China's history.

However, there is a cyclical or dual sided nature to the society. In all this modern brilliance this form of Socialism has created a larger class divide than most non socialist nations.
The communist ideals and links to the actual ideology of a communist body can now be made out as just a label. The income equality of mainland China is huge and the gap is only increasing as the nation continues to grow.

The continual economic and social reform since the events of 1989 have generated opportunities that the four and a half or likely more millionaire's and 373 or more billionaire's in China have taken advantage of.

This wealth and these individuals have simulated growth on both the micro and macro scale at all parts of China. With this wealth there is very much an understanding that to be an influential stake holder in China you must align with the government.

Those that do not support the State not only defy one of the remaining communist principles of 'state first' but they will find themselves in trouble. If they are wealthy individuals they will quickly find themselves unsuccessful or labelled and tried for corruption, embezzlement, bribery or worse. Which is very different to the systems of the West where wealth is a barrier to reprimand.
The statistics of wealth distribution across modern Chinese society is also very different to the rest of the world. In China the richest one percent own one third of the wealth, where as in America the richest own approx 40 percent.

This is seen in actual cultural policy that has one purpose, to keep the wealthy as low key as possible and to keep the poor content. If not then there could be serious instability and a dynamic shift in political and private sector power.

ART

There is no other sector that relays the physical change in culture than Art. This Chinese Art sector is booming. China has long been a hub of Artistic innovation which went underground in the hardcore communist era. The nation has since gone from the home of copycat works, duplications and con pieces to aristocratic levels of refined creativity and vision.

This change is owed to the Government efforts. They managed to evolve what 'made in China' means on all levels, from cheap and poorly made products in other industries to replica oil paintings. This crackdown has killed the 'fake' artistic scenes which churned out famous works for cents.
With a third of global art sales now taking place in China the evolution of culture has almost certainly been cyclical. With a large educated middle class and interested younger buyers Art has taken over.

If you go to any of the Art Schools in Europe or America they will be dominated by Chinese students. This influx of Chinese nationals are learning the markets, the trade and building their knowledge and taking it back home. This has allowed numerous large scale auction houses to pop up in rapid time. This new generation of individuals educated abroad and even within China only form a tiny niche of the greater society. But when compared to scale and the ratios, the amount of vested individuals interested in Art within China surpass the same niche of any other developed nation.

THE NOUVEAU RICHE

There is a risk of being rich in China, but it is not nearly as big as the risk of living in poverty. Only 1 percent of Chinese nationals would say that luxury products are superficial and China is now the leading market for all luxury brands. Within this expanding group of the newly rich families and individuals there is a growing disparity between the generations as well. The first generation money makers have since passed their wealth onto their children and increasingly grandchildren.

As the saying goes 'money makes money' this niche of society is now afforded time and leisure, even whilst their fortunes grow which has been illegal in past systems of Chinese Government.
This has given rise to the nouveau riche image that most Westerners accustom to new money. If you don't quite follow it is well worth learning the saying "Money speaks, wealth whispers." In other words the billionaires of history don't need to show their cash off, this is for the individuals that have recently risen from poverty.

In China, those towards the top of the middle class and upwards drive the luxury good, leisure and hospitality sector and demand. The proportionate scale of this niche is absolutely massive and as such competition is common. There is also the factor that if you are successful you have the right to shout about it. This overt celebration is deemed a positive quality by many in China. In many workplaces there is also the common attitude that to really work hard you must of course play hard, which in turn fuel surface level purchases – which in turn lend to the image of the Nouveau Riche.

THE IMPORTANCE OF 'FACE'
IN MODERN CHINA

Increasingly the culture of China distinguishes people by their income. With this societal value placed on earnings the word face has become prominent. Image, respect, opinion and others intentions ie. how much they are willing to do for you, and overall ones level in society is known as 'face.' If you are aspiring to join those who care about face there is a very clear pattern, and it is important to be aware of if you are doing business in China. Your social network, your fashion sense, your philanthropic efforts, the festivals, parties, concerts and sphere of your business attentions all lead to face value.

What you truly enjoy doing is apparently insignificant as the opportunities presented in that specific yacht club, spa complex or polo team is where the real value is derived. The modern and ambitious Chinese never disconnect from business. Whatever activity, past time, or social event they are attending. The concept of face and how you can work it in your favour, however indirectly or subversively is the real agenda.

The Modern Chinese Migration has been underway since the 1990's. This is of course the migration of millionaires to the capital markets of the rest of the world, often with more favourable tax systems. The Taiwanese and Hong Kong migrants paved the way for this most recent cultural norm of leaving China when you have enough money. Of course this is not the first economic-cultural migration in China. In every major city across the planet there is a small area, close to the centre with the title of 'China Town.'

TECH INTERCONNECTED SOCIETY

Technology in China is now beyond the point of being a luxury or want. It is very much a part of society and it's role is now essential. If you haven't walked the streets of any major city in China and seen the thousands of people on their phone, then imagine a western city only with a far greater smartphone dependency.
The idea of mobile phone activity becoming habitual or even addictive is non existent in China. If you are not using your mobile as the infrastructure forces you will miss out or be at a disadvantage.
The really unique thing is this is the case across the whole spectrum of modern Chinese society. Whether it is the fuerdai (trust fund children) or the farmer coming in for market day, all are on their mobiles. This has been due to a few social, governmental and plain old natural progressions over the time since smartphones became popular.

In short, Chinese nationals are using Chinese made smartphones with Chinese support networks to power near enough every aspect of their lives. This has led to a near cashless society. Dirty coins and notes are a thing of the past and every monetary transaction from buying a car to using the rail system can be made with one of three main tools.

Alipay
The mother company of this payment method is Alibaba. The Chinese equivalent of ebay and amazon combined. Alipay like taobao and wechat pay takes a mere second for the purchaser to complete their transaction by scanning a QR code.

Taobao
Taobao is the largest e-commerce site in the world. The mobile app allows the user to pay for any good or service in the modern cities of China much like Alipay.

Wechat pay
If you are young, doing business or new to China then it is apparently impossible to fully take part in the society and culture if you do not have wechat. Wechat is the largest social media platform and payment method in China but so much more. It is all the social media of the west rolled into one and then injected with steroids.

Every facet of a normal persons existence is now co-ordinated through technology or their smartphone. This can be coordinating a business meeting to booking a doctors appointment. The first step in China is now virtual. The lines between what is going on in the cybersphere and reality are blurring as technology advances, which makes for a very interesting time.

The rest of the world will follow the technological infrastructure of modern China. It is moulding a new society the use of QR scans, the integration of social media, cookies, data and surveillance into the real world is something we can see taking shape in the West.

Of course the smart phone interaction and its uses are just one aspect of tech in modern China's society. Facial recognition is for the most part a positive, but the really futuristic aspects of society, that are now commonplace in large Chinese cities are the employee-less stores. Like a step in vending machine these small shops are open 24/7 and incredibly efficient.

Tech is already ingrained in modern China but it's only just getting started. This is largely due to the Governments care and support of the tech giants that foster innovation on the macro scale. It is also partly down to the Chinese people who vare technologically adept.

In the next few years we will see the nation push for a superior high tech manufacturing sector, nation wide 5G and the rise of the digital silk road, all as these mega corporations push for international presence or domination.

THE MIDDLE CLASS AND THE SUBURBS

If you still think America is the homeland of suburbia then think again. The lands of golf courses, gated communities, miles of estates and all that comes with them is in China. The Chinese Middle Class is the same size as the whole of America with an extra 50 million more people.

The semi urban middle class of China has financed the development of once rural areas around the biggest cities into luxury flats or detached and semi detached housing estates. There are areas in Beijing, Shanghai and the other major cities which surpass the luxury of Beverly Hills or the gated communities in Europe.

It is fascinating to observe the many styles and engineering of such immense projects all over China. There is also one massive difference between China and the rest of the word when it comes to Property. When you reach the middle class you normally want to buy your home, but in China the idea of freehold is non existent. In China an individual cannot privately own land but may obtain transferable land-use rights for a number of years for a fee.

However individuals may own private residential houses and apartments on the land ("home ownership"), but not this land, which the buildings are situated up. Therefore the State never really loses control and you are forced into the typical 70 year lease of the land.

THE LAY OF THE LAND

China is comprised of 4 Municipalities, 23 Provinces, 5 Autonomous regions and 2 Special Administrative Regions. The Four Municipalities are – Beijing, Chongqing, Shanghai and Tianjin. The 23 Provinces are Anhui, Fujian, Gansu, Guangdon, Guizhou, Hainan, Hebei, Heilongjiang, Henan, Hubei, Hunan, Jiangsu, Jiangxi, Jilin, Liaoning,

Qinghai, Shaanxi, Shandong, Sichuan, Yunnan, Zheijang and some would argue Taiwan, some would argue not Taiwan.
China's five autonomous regions are Guanxi, Inner Mongolia, Ningxia, Tibet, Xinjiang.

The Two Special administrative regions are Hong Kong and Macau. It is also worth noting that there are five special economic zones in modern China. These areas have special rulings and an environment to inhibit rapid growth. They are the cities of Xiamen, Shantou, Shenzhen, Zhuhai and Kashgar. In addition to this there are 15 free-trade zones, 32 state level economic and technological development zones and 53 new and high tech industrial development zones in a number of medium and large sized cities. China also has a series of open coastal cities, specifically designed in the eighties to act as windows and accelerators for foreign trade. They have since turned into 14 massive and highly productive economic areas. These cities are Dalian, Qinhuangdao, Tianjin, Yantai, Qingdao, Lianyungang, Nantong, Shanghai, Ningbo, Wenzhou, Fuzhou, Guangzhou, Zhanjiang, and Beihai.

MODERN CHINA AND ITS RELATION TO TCM

Despite adopting and innovating on all that is new in modern China, traditional Chinese medicine remains prominent. More so, these ancient medicines, treatments and reliefs are spreading across the globe on the same scale as many other Chinese exports. In the West Chinese medicine has already been a made a case of hearsay. If you are a firm believer or a sceptic then all you have to do is visit one of the shops in any China Town or resort to an online purchase to have a go.
Now, internal and external to China these medicines are merging with modern pharmacies and classic medications, which is the best route to take.
The two types of 'healing' of East and West, when merged together can compliment one another to better the chances of success.
Saying this, Chinese medicine, even the most modern forms of it, still has much to be proven. The scale of the demand within China, and now overseas is putting an unnecessary and destructive strain on natural resources.

The practices of acupuncture, cupping, various massage methods, qi, meridians die-da and physical treatments, whilst not proven in scientific theory do work a lot of good in reality.

Where there is cause for concern in Modern China is in the area of Chinese Herbology/Herbal Medicines, Food therapy and Traditions.

Chinese Herbology/Herbal Medicines

Despite the name employs less herbs and more animal and sometimes even human body parts. It is perhaps the one area of this logical and clearly effective style of medicine that gives it all a bad perception. The rest of the world increasingly overlook the positives of the herbs and directly to the shamanic use of animal and human parts. The human or animal parts accompany the plant based ingredients that do have results when it comes to usage, which then gets associated to neither positive or negative, but definitely destructive regarding animal and human parts.

Because 'face' and status is now a part of the Chinese elite, the middle class and the culture of Chinese medicine, some truly barbaric practices have quickly become normalised. The new purchasing power of many individuals has led to the rise of demand and profiting from the ingredients of Chinese medicine. This has caused several catastrophes. Chinese medicine when it comes to the use of animal parts is cruelty on an industrial scale. When you are in China, as a national or a visitor your mind is typically not on this part of society. Most people are either too busy or just in awe of the culture, the people and the society to notice (or think about) this niche area of Chinese Medicine.

The average persons mind is not on the Rhino horn, shark fin, manta ray and 45 plus other common components of the medicine and market. Despite a small visual presence there is also the consumer habits of this whole movement. If we overlook the obvious dangers and unnecessary pain of wet markets, shark fin soup and objectify the demand we can see the scale.

Sharkfin Soup

Shark fin soup is traditionally a wedding dish or occasional dish at celebrations. It is a dish many modern Chinese will eat once in their life or only a few times. But when the nation is as large as China it is simply too too large to support this consumer activity without disturbing the whole planets balance and eco systems. There are 50-100 million weddings a year in China and this 'occasional' meal or medicine suddenly becomes detrimental to the whole planets balance and health. Additionally those who supply the demand practice 'finning' where fishermen cut the fins off live sharks and throw the remaining fish back to die. With this level of demand 12,000 sharks are killed every single hour across the globe. This accounts to 100 million sharks killed every year to support this one aspect of tradition or culture.

Rhino Horn and Ivory
The corruption of African states and willingness of poachers have met the demand for Rhino horn in mainland China. Resulting in the extinction and endangerment of every single Rhino breed. Rhino horn is made up of Keratin, the same as human fingernails.

Ivory from elephants is also in huge demand, both as a form of social status by having it as an ornament and as a component for medicine. The demand for elephant tusks is now the largest contributor to this species decline. Turtles, Tigers, Tortoises, Bats, Snakes and near enough every other living creature has a use in Chinese medicine, despite modern scientific testing proving these parts have no clinical or physical effects.

If modern China and those supporting these businesses continue there is only two answers to avoid further extinctions. To stop consuming, to begin cell agriculture or start breeding schemes are the only future avenues China can take. At present those animals which are not hunted or farmed in squalid and inhumane conditions, to then be sold in the notorious wet markets are poached around the planet. There is also the aspect of human body parts and usage in this area of Chinese medicine. Whilst most of the following are not in use, many recipes for medicine remain that include bones, fingernail, hairs, dandruff, earwax, impurities on the teeth, faeces, urine, sweat and organs. Of the medicines using human parts the most prominent in modern China is dried human placenta. Of all the Traditional Medicines it is the ones considered to be fringe movements in mainland China that prove most beneficial. The practices of cupping, gua-sha and die-da all do good and can heal ailments or health issues.

Coincidently they are also the practices that do not involve food therapy.

Fundamental Plants in Chinese Herbology

Perhaps the biggest threat to Chinese society is the scale of the consumer demands. Even small one time purchases of niche items are in demand on a scale that is too large. The following list is of the fundamental Chinese Herbs for traditional therapy and their usage.

For the budding entrepreneurs reading this a valuable and beneficial startup idea would be to employ vertical farming methods to these plants in an urban setting.

HERBS

Chinese, American and Siberian Ginseng

Ginseng is used to improve strength, increase blood volume, promote life and appetite. It is also prescribed for decreasing weakness, rectifying deficient qi patterns and assisting with anaemia and impotence.

Gingko

In the search for new therapeutic solutions to address an increasing number of multidrug-resistant bacterial pathogens, secondary metabolites from plants have proven to be a rich source of antimicrobial compounds

Mushrooms

Used over the past two millennia Mushrooms are both nutritional and interlinked with herbal medicine applications. They have been employed to boost well-being and longevity.

Wolfberry

Used for treating "yin deficiency" in the liver and kidney. This dried fruit is commonly prepared in a 6–15 g dose and taken twice or thrice daily.

Dan Gui

Dang Gui is one of the most common herbs in the Chinese herbal medicine system. It is primarily known as a "women's herb," though many men take it as well. It known to be a superior blood tonic.

Astragalus – Huang Qi

Astragalus is a herbal supplement that has been utilised for centuries in traditional Chinese medicine. It's reported to enhance the immune system and reduce inflammation. It is also used to help treat heart conditions, kidney disease and more.

Atractylodes

Atractylodes is used with other herbs for treating lung cancer (ninjin-yoei-to) and complications of dialysis, a mechanical method for "cleaning the blood" when the kidneys have failed (shenling baizhu san.)

Bupleurum

Used in a herbal formula for treating a blood disorder called thrombocytopenic purpura and to treat several chronic liver diseases such as hepatitis.

Cinnamon

A prized herb in China, Cinnamon is used to warm the body and promote blood circulation.

Coptis Chinensis

Coptis Chinensis or Chinese Goldthread contains several compounds thought to enhance health, including a salt known as berberine.

Ginger

Considered to be a warming herb and act specifically on the lungs, spleen and stomach; Ginger is a qi tonic and therefore promotes circulation and treats phlegm in the lungs accompanied with cough. The elderly also benefit from it treating joint pain in cold weather.

Liquorice

Liquorice root is one of the 50 fundamental herbs used in traditional Chinese medicine, where it has the name Gancao to harmonize other herbs and reduce the harsh effects of other herbs.

Ephedra

Ephedra, also named Ma Huang, is a herb that has been used in Traditional Chinese Medicine for more than 5,000 years, primarily to treat asthma, bronchitis, and hay fever. It is also prescribed for symptoms of cold and flu, including nasal congestion, cough, fever, and chills.

Peony

Dried Peony root is used to treat liver abnormalities, improve blood circulation and ease women's menstruation pains. One of the primary varieties of tree peonies is Phoenix White, which is also cultivated for it's beautiful flowers.

Rehmannia

Rehmannia is used to treat diabetes, metabolic syndrome, obesity, kidney disease, chronic obstructive pulmonary disease, "tired blood" (anemia), fever, weakened bones (osteoporosis), rheumatoid arthritis (RA), and allergies.

Rhubarb

Rhubarbs has been studied for the management of GI and renal function disorders, and for a treatment of hyperlipidemia, cancer, and acute ischemic stroke.

Salvia

Used in Chinese medicine to treat vascular disease. According to Chinese medicine theory, Danshen promotes blood flow and resolves blood stasis.

CUISINE, CULTURE AND HOSPITALITY

As Westerners or foreigners our perception of Chinese food is flawed, especially when it comes to modern China. Even if you live in one of the major Chinese cities there is a good chance of your perception being distorted by these modernised hubs which tailor to a new demand.

The most revered and notable Cuisines are -Chuan representing the West, Lu, representing the North and Yue and Huaiyang representing the South and East. The modern dynamic has evolved and built on these four traditional cuisines. It is widely accepted that there are eight main cuisines of modern Chinese, all with various offshoots or niches in modern China.

They are;

Anhui - 徽菜; Huīcài

Anhui is simplicity, or as simple as it gets in modern China. Braising and stewing takes precedence over frying or stir fry, which is popular in all the other cuisines. Anhui cuisine consists of three styles, that of the Yangtze river, The Huai River and the Southern Anhui region.

The reason for Anhui's difference in cooking style and preparation is down to the geography of the area it originated from. Anhui is still very natural, with plenty of fields and forest not put to work as farms. It is very similar to the biosphere of Europe and the diets of those in the coniferous regions. Anhui utilizes pigeon, partridge and plenty of herbs. Anhui is also the rumoured birthplace of Tofu, during the Han dynasty in 206bc to 220ad. From it's creation and adoption over the Asian and now European and American continents the likes of stinky tofu and hairy tofu are household dishes. Common Anhui ingredients include stinky mandarin fish, fried hairy tofu, steamed partridge, stewed bamboo shoots, stewed pigeon and chop suey.

Cantonese - 粤菜; Yuècài

Guangzhou or 'Canton City' is the central hub of Cantonese cuisine. From the outsiders perspective Cantonese is what we really think of when it comes to Chinese food. Cantonese utilises the methods of steaming, stir frying and roasting to cook it's sweet and sour dishes. As a trading hub Guangzhou has enabled chefs to adopt an enormous amount of ingredients into the dishes. Dim sum, duck, chicken and pork are the classics, but Cantonese is not a wasteful cuisine, what were once leftovers are now delicacies. The likes of offal, chicken feet, ducks tongue, frog legs, snakes and many more niche meats are used to great success. Cantonese is also a fast cuisine, with it's go to methods of steaming, shallow frying, double steaming, deep frying, braising and stir fry. It is also the most common street food. Cantonese, due to it's nature and utility is now employed in every city and will be a staple to the farmers market. The final focus of Cantonese cuisine is in the freshness of ingredients used, which is a top priority. The dishes should be balanced, not greasy and aromatic.

Fujian - 闽菜; Mǐncài

Also known as Hokkien, Fujianese, or Min Cuisine this notable food group is primarily soup based. The capital of Fujian food is Fuzhou, in the Fujian Province which has a history of ample sea and forest based foods. Fujian is all about bring out the original flavour of the ingredients. It is light, flavourful and soft with other ingredients complimenting rather than masking the main body of the dish. The coastal and mountainous region of Fushan has enabled woodland and coastal delicacies to merge together. Traditional chefs of Fujianese will say it is unacceptable for a dish to be served without a broth or soup. There is a whole subculture around the use of broths and soups as an instrument of flavour. This has stemmed into the use and mixing of regional ingredients like mushrooms, bamboo shoots, shellfish and turtles.

The main methods of cooking this cuisine is braising, steaming, boiling and stewing. This is second to the emphasis placed on the chefs technique and their knife skills. Taiwan has quickly emerged as a hub of Fujanese food. The majority of Taiwanese have ancestral ties to Fujian province in mainland China and the cuisine migrated with them. In modern Fujianese the use of 'shrimp oil' is an absolute necessity. This oil is in fact fermented fish sauce and used alongside oyster, crab and shrimp. Peanuts are also a staple, being used in main dishes and deserts. Used as a garnish, a braise, stir fry and soups the taste of peanuts is a tell-tell sign of Fujianese. Fujian consists of three main styles, Fuzhou, Southern Fujian and Western Fujian. Fuzhou employs both sweet and sour tastes and is much lighter when compared to the other styles. Fuzhou is the prominent style of Fujianese soups, fermented fish sauce and red rice. Souther Fujian is closer to Japanese and South East Asian cuisine. Using lots of sugars, spices and slow cooking it brings out a stronger flavour. Many of the dishes, irrespective of it being pork, pork offal, beef, chicken, duck, seafood and vegetables are served with dipping sauces. The taste is not just stronger but typically oilier and saltier. This style of cooking is now officially under the definition of Taiwanese cuisine. Western

Fujian is the slightest of the styles. It is saltier and oilier than the other Fujian methods and employs gentler cooking methods.

Hunan - 湘菜; Xiāngcài

Hunanese or Xiang cuisine is rich, fresh, aromatic and spicy. Specifically it is hot, sour and fairly similar to Sichuan cuisine, except more fragrant and stronger in taste. It also relies more on lemons and the use of crunchy vegetables to accompany the stewed, fried, pot roasted, braised or smoked main dishes. The ingredients do vary and with the region being massively agricultural there is a surplus of goods that can be used in dishes. Hunanese is also one of the youngest cooking styles. It dates back to the 17th century and was an amalgamation of much older methods. Hunanese consists of three main styles, Xiang River Style, Gongting Lake style and the Western Hunan style. Because Sichuan and Hunanese often get mistaken for one another, when you talk about or look at the dish remember that Sichuan is spicy and numbing. It is deliberately dry and hot to taste. Whilst just as oily as Sichuan, Hunanese is simpler. It's tastes are less complex and more deliberate. Hunanese cuisine is also dictated by the seasons and available food groups. In the summer dishes will be served cold and laid out very similar to Arabic platters. In the winter the most popular choice is the hot pot with the epitome of Hunan Hotpot being the yuanyang huoguo (鸳鸯火锅; 鴛鴦火鍋) where one half is served hot and the other half mild.

Jiangsu - 苏菜; Sūcài

One of the most well known of the eight cuisines is Jiangsu or Su cuisine. It is a difficult to cook well and is therefore rewarded with many of the top chefs having a legendary status. It is also the most frowned upon of the big eight cuisines, based on the fact that many dishes contain live aquatic ingredients. Therefore much of the skill that goes into precision carving, perfect cooking of the vegetables and the light fresh taste that this style preserves are overlooked. Jiangsu ingredients are typically ocean or coastal based with some coming from further inland. There is a great deal of focus in the ingredients matching, both in colour and size, with a soup to compliment the dish being a common feature. In modern China the most notable hub of Jiangsu was Shanghai, with modern Shanghai cuisine now being classed as Jiangsu. Jiangsu is actually made up of several sub regional styles. These are based on the proximity to freshwater sources and the ingredients incorporated.

Shandong - 鲁菜; Lǔcài

Shandong is one of the most influential of all China's cuisines. It is what a full English breakfast is to the British = a traditional and favourite staple that hasn't been mass exported. The main methods of cooking Shandongese foods are Bao, Liu, Pa, Kao, Zhu and utilising Sugar and honey to crystallize. For a quick understanding of these methods they are;

Bao is quick frying, Liu is quick frying with corn flour, Pa is stewing, Kao is roasting and Zhu is boiling. On top of these methods Shandong is also divided into two styles based on the regions. Jinan and Jiaodong. All Shandong should be known for it's freshness, light aroma and richness.

The Jinan style's geography is Jinan, Dezhou, Tai'an and surrounding regions who's dishes are notable for their use of soup.

The Jiadong style encompasses all the dishes of the Eastern Shandong region. Fushan, Qindao, Yantai and the surrounding regions are included and know for their use of seafood and light tastes.

Sichuan - 川菜; Chuāncài

Sichuan cuisine is the biggest, most popular, influential, and main cuisine of China and therefore the world. Sichuan is easily identifiable once you have had it a few times. It has bold, pungent and spicy flavours with a strong tendency for cooks to use chilli, garlic, broad bean sauce and unique Sichuan ingredients of mustard and ginger.

The reason for it's distinct variation from all other Chinese cuisine is down to the Silk road. Middle Eastern crops, spices and styles were introduced to the culture. Since then it has continued to adopt other geographic and international ingredients. Sichuan cuisine has taken the best ingredients, spices and tasteful crops from India, Mexico, the America's and South East Asia. The geography where Sichuan cuisine resides is also abundant in natural resources. It is this abundance that has allowed individuals to enjoy the hot and spice whilst also having cold dishes at the same meal. Sichuan cuisine is affords seven basic flavours. Sour, pungent, hot, sweet, bitter, aromatic and salty and these are then divided into one of five Sichuan meal types. Sumptuous banquet, ordinary banquet, popularised food and household-style food and snacks. It is the Sichuan style that is popularised in Chinese American households but not Chinese American restaurants.

Zhejiang - 浙菜; Zhècài

Many view Zheijang cuisine as the most traditional or classic form of Chinese cuisine. Whilst not the oldest or most recognisable food style to an outsider, it is pretty central to modern China. Zheijang Province is South of Shanghai and centred in Hangzhou, one of China's historical capitals. It has a fresh and soft flavour with a mellow fragrance and consists of at least three styles from the three major cities of the province. These styles, like much of the rest of China, have overlapped with other cuisines to form a multi faceted scene. The true styles remain; The Hanzhou Style, the Shaoxing style, Ningbo and Wenzhou which shows the morphing of recipes and cuisines as some also list it under Fujian.

THE FUTURE OF CHINESE CUISINE

Chinese cuisines are ever changing and evolving. The Chinese people are unique in the fact that boundaries do not exist when it comes to feeding themselves. This 'unlocked' approach to what is food and what could potentially be food has allowed for a vast and diverse range. This combined with the modernisation of the nation, the old breed of Chinese chefs becoming rarer and rarer, and the lack of recipes being passed down in families has forced change too. Whilst the main cuisines listed above set guidelines and rules the future of Chinese cuisine will evolve even more. The traditional foods, environmental consequences and consumer trends will force another mutation to the original recipes and foods. Saying this, these new ingredients will be sourced according to colour, smell, taste and then the meaning, appearance and nutrition, thus allowing them to fit the bill and be made Chinese cuisine.

TEA

There is a legend that says in the year 2737bc the Chinese Emperor Shen Nung watch a green leaf get blown into a bowl of boiling water. The leaf coloured the water and created what became known as tea. Since the first cup was drunk by the Emperor or one of his subjects, the herbs used to create flavoursome beverages has since been refined. Since then, Tea has and will remain a critical pillar of Chinese culture. It is used in herbal medicine, cooking, as a nutrient, as a past time and generally acceptable to drink with anything. In every community in China, and near enough every household Tea leaves and the individual ceremonies to serve them can be found. Whether you are rich or poor, in the countryside or the technological hub of the world, hot tea will be nearby. In China the Tea types are traditionally Green Tea, Black Tea, Oolong Tea, White Tea, Yellow Tea and Dark Tea.

Oolong Tea is the 'most Chinese' of these varieties as Oolong leaves only grows in the Anxi and Fujian regions. Oolong is also different to other tea types based on the effects it has on the body. Oolong Tea is very healthy, it is good for the heart, brain, bone and teeth. It may also boost your metabolism, decrease the risk of developing type 2 diabetes and protect against certain types of cancer.

Tea, whatever the type has long been regarded as one of the seven daily necessities, the others being firewood, rice, oil, salt, soy sauce, and vinegar. It seems even as China Westernises and becomes near futuristic in some parts, the culture and drinking of tea is set to stay.

CLIMATE

The biomes of China vary to create a truly diverse landscape. Due to the sheer landmass and human elements the biomes of the nation are more similar to the type of disparity and comparisons we see on a continental level. A biome is the flora and fauna (plants and animals) that make up a specific habitat. All of these factors, combined with human activity effect the biomes and climate of the region. China's climate and regions can be broken down as such -

Northern China
With an Arid and Semi Arid Continental Climate temperatures rarely exceed 21c in the Summer but can drop to –35c in the Winter. Both North and North West China is comprised of Desert and Steppes.

North West China
With Semi Arid and Highland Climates the deserts of this region allow for an average of 23c in the urban settings in the Summer, (albeit much hotter in the deserts.) The area is recorded to reach –45c in the winter at night.

North East China
A mix of cool temperature climates, cold winters and humid monsoons make the winters harsh and the summers hot. Temperatures in the winter can reach –20c and the summers more that 26c on average.

Central China
Central China is predominantly half and half, it is half Highland Climate and half Sub Tropical Monsoon climate. The winters are at least –30c and the summers 25c. Central, Western and Southern

China is made up of high mountain vegetation and Tropical Monsoon Forest.

Southern and South Eastern China
Southern China is a mix of tropical, tropical monsoon, subtropical monsoon and in the true South even dry winters. The winters are typically 8c and the summers 28c.

Eastern China
Eastern China is both coastal and a mix of subtropical, semi arid and monsoon climates. The temperatures have been changing over the last few years but summers are hot (more than 25c) and winters are reasonable, with it getting colder the more north you go. Eastern China contains the nations shorelines, temperate deciduous forest and tropical monsoon forests. The increasing human activity is notable in its destruction and pollution of the natural areas of China.

Ancient Chinese cities and people harnessed the best of nature by working with it, but since the 1950's the 'urbanise and industrialise at all costs' attitude is close to doing near irreversible damage.

MILITARY AND REGIONAL SECURITY

Regional stability of China is as old the most ancient settlement. It is fair to say the nation we recognize today started a new era of regional stability and reasonable military expansion, since the 1950's. Under the Western evacuation by order of Mao in 1949 all foreigners left China. This ranged from the Christian priests to car dealers. It is in this era of isolation when the nation reformed, that we see a new era of Chinese military power. The People's Army of that time formed the foundation of the modern military we see today, with an army of a million plus which continues to expand.

The modern military is a large and powerful segment of the middle class within China today. Within these communities and military families the classic communist principles are still at large, and a basis of the organisations ethos.

This is the final area where the misconstrued image of yellow peril and fear of China remains. In 1960's America it was this fear and suspicion of China that resulted in the US punishing or expelling all members of the Government in Washington who spoke Chinese. It is this Sino-American military competition or disdain for one another that has led to the cold war style stand-off in the Pacific today. Where China has undergone an era of reverse colonisation since Mao, using soft strategies of industry, culture and trade to become a world power it is America that remains on top when it comes to military might.

The US Navy has dominated the Pacific's surface, air and the depths since the second world war for strategic purposes. It is only now where we see tension arise as the new China expands. China observes the South China Sea and parts of the Pacific as it's own. This goes beyond the understood coastal and maritime waters under rightful ownership. The US Military presence in these areas has also increased, subversively and intelligently. The reason why is a question only the top of the command chain can answer. The reality is it looks like the US is encircling China through surveillance, increasing military bases, defence, attack capabilities and overall force presence.

China and the US are also part of collective agreements that would result in total war across the planet, if they ever did go to War. The United States is part of NATO and the Chinese part of the Shanghai Cooperation Organisation. If politics and pursuing action ever did go sour then the following nuclear winter would mean absolutely no winner, let alone jostling for places as world number one.

The Media, Propaganda and activities in the cybersphere of both nations are the most active area's. With massive hacking campaigns taking place daily. However the land, sea air and space operations are accelerating as well. The space race is alive today and the Arms sector increasing.

The Arms Industry
China is the second largest Arms producer on the planet and second largest investor in defence. The culture and nature of the national agenda may not see it overtake the US in either of these areas, but China does utilise soft power more effectively. The Arms Industry is sufficient and continues to grow, but in typical Chinese

manufacturing fashion. There are at least two "munitions cities" in China.

Without naming names there is one such company that has been developed and equates to the size of a small city. It's red soil and pollution levels are so high the setting is like that of a foreign planet.

The scale of these weapons manufacturing facilities are so large, and so industrial it is a mix of terrifying and fascinating. With increasing security and the protection of such sites improving it is unlikely that you will be able to visit.

ANTHROPOLOGY, BIOLOGY AND GENETIC HISTORY

This is a topical and touchy subject, but one we must delve into for a better understanding of the modern nation. In modern Europe and America the partnership of all people, whatever their cultural or ethnic background is commonplace.

In China it is distinctly not the case. Whilst you might think that it is due to the sheer lack of migration when it is studied down to the quantitative percentage and ratios this 'mixing' is not so prominent. Without causing offence there is no way of going into the how or why behind it. Instead we must look at the anthropology and biology of modern China.

We are not talking about race but the hard science, many experts now believe race to be a historic categorisation and false. It takes ten generations for a genetic line of people to adapt to their environment. Meaning in ten generations your offspring can have evolved to the African continent and have the features to better cope or vice versa.

It goes for all the 'races' and is the case with modern China. The most common misconception on this topic is that everyone in China follows the same line of genetics and culture. Whilst the majority of nationals are Han Chinese, with the latest surveys predicting 90% of the nation, they are in fact massively diverse.

140

Getting straight into it the reason behind the skin tones have evolved just like every other 'race' on earth. Soil, minerals, the environment, conditions, the sky and level of the suns brightness all determine eye and skin colour.

This of course can be seen in the varying shades of both the Han and minority ethnic groups, determined by the region their families and ancestors settled in. Height and build of the modern Chinese is also changing. Traditionally the typical Chinese national is slim, prone to endurance and overall fairly healthy due to the cuisine and diet.

Height is determined due to genetics, food groups prominent in the diet and quality of the water. Similar to early Europeans and Africans those ethnic groups located near rivers with high calcium levels grew taller. The modern mega cities are also changing the physical structure of people, and perhaps not for the best.

Access to new foods, cheaper ingredients and higher fat contents, combined with the easier lifestyles is weakening the biology, but this is the same for everywhere in the world. Finally and perhaps most carefully there is the factor of the Asian eye type, specifically the East Asian. Many people are not aware of the actual facts and provenance which is why this is essential to know.

When early man left Africa the modern day Europeans settled to the North and West of the Caucus mountain range. Then the ice age occurred trapping and separating them from the rest of the world. They developed whiter and lighter features and lived in rich forests, grasslands and mountains for millennia.

The ancestors of modern Asians settled in the Middle East, South Asia (India) and evolved to better suit the deserts, jungles and heat. The East Asians, of genetic similarity to the Han and other Eastern nations crossed at least seven deserts including the Taklamakan and Gobi. In addition to this they crossed the ice sheets of Northern Mongolia and the harsh conditions of Northern China, Russia, Mongolia and China.

Because of these harsh conditions, brightness and huge wind levels the eyelid evolved to reduce glare and prevent blindness. This is known as the epicanthic fold. Much of Eastern Russia, Korea, Japan and Eastern China were connected to Alaska via an ice Shelf. This would allow further migration into America and link the Native American tribes with these early people.

Lactose Intolerance is prevalent in China and much of Asia. Historically the cultural groups that farmed the nation did not breed cattle, with the landscape being more suitable for pig sheep, goat or chicken farming. As such the stomach and ability to consume lactose or milk based produce never took form and has left many with an intolerance for these goods.

Another notable biological difference is in alcohol consumption and food portions. Specifically when it comes to alcohol the East Asian stomach became tailored to process wine, rice and other prominent cuisines. The Caucasian and Eurasian both developed the ability to process wheat, grain, oats, beer and bread earlier than that of the African or other continents, but struggled with spices. It is an interesting biological aspect to the modern nation and society; And something that we see even to this day within the timeline of globalisation.

TEACHING AND EDUCATION

At bachelors level many in China still favour the United Kingdom and United States, if their families can afford it. The Universities in China provide varying degrees at varying levels on a truly enormous scale. The competition of entry to a Chinese University is also fierce, in many ways the culture promotes it as the most important step in a young persons life.
Modern China has a mix of the Western education structure but with Chinese academia and work ethic. The Universities have also led to a more internationalised China with foreign students and lecturers now playing important roles.

Beyond undergraduate level masters and doctoral studies take on a more constructive approach with subject matter being typically practical, not theoretical. Of course there are numerous campuses offering significant and very good courses or studies in liberal arts and 'left side of the brain subjects' like the humanities, but where Chinese education excels is in the fields of science, engineering, mathematics and economics.

At high school level there is a growing divide between a fantastic education and a poor one. It all depends on status and economic position. Private school fees are rising in China and offering both an American style diploma or a Chinese style diploma. Within both private and public institutions learning difficulties and autism are not recognised, let alone tailored too. A child with ADHD or any other condition determined with psychometric testing is not considered to have a genuine problem but to be a trickster or lazy.

This puts more strain on the students, where the Chinese side of the high school education is memory focused, rather than critical thinking based. Consequently, the families pressure combined with goals of the school is all channelled into the role of the teacher. Educational reform and a change to it's policy within China is imminent. The system is so vast that even with regional oversight the bottom line is still vastly disproportionate, in both private and state schools.

Teaching in China, specifically teaching English as a native speaker has turned into a lucrative career, with it's own fair share of imposters.

Whether your taking classes part time at a local school, teaching in lectures at a University or privately tutoring, the returns are great, and the poorly qualified 'imposters' are on the increase.
In modern China parents will not cut short at the cost of education, in fact it is an area they are often willing to overpay for. Within the curriculum of China there is also a distinct lack of weighted arguments and critical analysis to both sides of all arguments. This ranges from subjects like history to art to politics. Without the education to teach the manner of thinking that is necessary for free

143

debate it acts as a form of chiselling the society from youth upwards to not counter argue.

The education also differs in China as there is more emphasis on memory and exams and not necessarily the interest to learn the subject out of interest. This could be a reason for the lack of all other education methods, except copy to perfection. Also in the West education has no "off limits" in a subject. Anything from sex education to questionable politics can be bought up and talked about in detail. In modern China this is less common, but something that will likely change with all the Chinese nationals educated abroad coming back and making a change.

THE CLASS SYSTEM

China is now a vertical class based society that holds the communist or socialist ideals close but not scrupulously. This begs the question about Communism, not the party but the ideals. Are they just a label in China now?

Consumerism seems to have more of an effect on your average person than Communist theory. The disparity between the wealthy and poor is truly incredible. Something as simple as etiquette or now normal behaviour shows the difference that even ten years can make.

It would not be wise to doubt the Communist Party as there will be indefinite order as they are so good at preventing, defending and protecting the state before problems arise, rather than reacting to them afterwards. But the class system within the society seems more vertical and steeped in levels that even semi-right wing nations.

If we take America for instance the media propagates racial tension to distract from the real divide – personal wealth and income. In ancient Rome there was also a strategy of 'Bread and Circuses' where the Emperor would throw a series of games in the colosseum. They would be so epic, and pull people in with free bread to distract the greater population from their problems of inequality. What is unique with China is there is not visible efforts being made to hide this feature of a class, other than the rich living humbly and doing their bit for the party.

NOTABLE LEADERS AND NATION SHAPERS

This chapter presents the profiles of some of China's greatest leaders. To understand the modern nation we must understand some of the people who helped shape it.

Zheng He / Ma He

Zheng He is perhaps ancient China's greatest mariner, explorer, diplomat, fleet admiral and court eunuch. He lived during China's early Ming dynasty and served the Ming Court. He was born a Muslim and named Ma He, his family would adopt the surname Zheng, granted by Emperor Yongle.

As he grew older so did his capacity in the Dynasty, his contribution to China as a whole lies in his expeditions and Command. Zheng led expeditionary treasure voyages across Southeast Asia, the Indian subcontinent, Western Asia and even East Africa. The voyages would bring back wealth and secure overseas political influence. On top of this they inspired hope in the Ming Dynasty, which ultimately became one of China's most technologically advanced and affluent Imperial Dynasties.

His vessels were unlike anything the world had ever seen. Operating from 1405 to 1433 they had four decks and were almost twice as long as any wooden ship ever recorded. Carrying hundreds of sailors, soldiers, merchants, diplomats and treasure they set the new standard for Asian Ocean supremacy.

Zheng would quickly become a favourite of the Yongle Emperor, who he would ultimately stay loyal too. In doing so Zheng would assist in the overthrow of the Jianwen Emperor and rise to the top of the Imperial hierarchy. He would spend his remaining years not at sea but as commander of the southern capital Nanjing.

Sun Yat-sen.

Sun Yat-sen lived between 1866 and 1925. He was a Chinese politician, physician and political philosopher who moulded the end of the Imperial Dynasty into the Republic of China. He is remembered for his ability to mould the perception and opinion of China's public and inspire confidence. He would go onto become the provisional President of the Republic of China and the first leader of the Kuomintang, or Nationalist Party of China.

He bred national pride, inspired trade and built a new free market with close connections to the Government administration. All of this built the foundation of the later left wing and communist emergence. Long before formation of a new nation Sun Yat-Sen came to prominence for his part in the toppling of the Qing dynasty. His part in the Xinhai Revolution was significant and won him favour amongst the masses, with many viewing him as one of the greatest leaders in both both mainland China and Taiwan today. The reality is very different, Sun spent most of his political life in exile. He was very much an impact player and would cause the initial change and move on. This can be seen in the successful revolution of 1911. Sun would lead the movement but resign as President of the newly founded Republic of China not soon after. In doing so he relinquished power and position to Yuan Shikai. Sun would exile in Japan for his own safety. His political and policy goals were fantastic, and known as 'The Three Principles of the People.' They were;

x) 民族主義, Mínzú Zhǔyì / NATIONALISM
x) 民權主義, Mínquán Zhǔyì / RIGHTS OF THE PEOPLE / DEMOCRACY

x) 民生主義, Mínshēng Zhǔyì / SOCIALISM/WELFARE

Sun would return to China and form a revolutionary government in the South. Warlords took control of the region and he wanted to reassert dominance of the new nation. At the same time he invited representatives of the Communist International to Canton, where they would restructure and organise the Party. They were successful and even formed a delicate alliance with the Chinese Communist Party. Sun died in 1925 of Gallbladder Cancer and would not live to see the Party unify under his successor.

Image of Sun Yat Sen

Xuanzang

Xuanzang lived in the era of the Tang Dynasty. He was a Chinese
Buddhist monk, scholar, traveller, and translator. His place in Chinese
history is significant as he travelled to India and returned with;
x) More than six hundred Mahayana and Hinayana texts
x) Seven statues of the Buddha
x) More than a hundred sarira relics.
In doing so he exponentially increased the understanding and
prominence of Buddhism in ancient China.

Su Song

Su Song lived between 1020–1101 during the Song Dynasty. He was
also known as Zirong and would become a prominent Chinese
polymath, scientist and statesman. He excelled in academia and
intellectual creation, specialising in mathematics, astronomy,
cartography, geography, horology, pharmacology, mineralogy,
metallurgy, zoology, botany, mechanical engineering, hydraulic
engineering, civil engineering, architecture, invention, art, poetry,
philosophy, antiquities, and statesmanship.

Su Song engineered the hydro-mechanical astronomical clock tower in
medieval Kaifeng. Su Song built on the creation of a Buddhist Monk named

Yi Xing and a Government Official, named Liang Lingzan. The pair had created and built the first escapement mechanism for a water powered armillary sphere. Su Song had adjusted the armillary sphere and became the first to be used with a mechanical clock drive. Su's clock tower also contained the oldest known endless power-transmitting chain drive, or in his own words a *tian tic* (天梯), or "celestial ladder." The clock tower had 133 different clock jacks which emitted sound for the hours. Su Song's written work about the clock tower, called *Xinyi Xiangfayao* (新儀象法要), has survived since its written form in 1092. It was printed by the Song Dynasty on a large scale in 1094. The clock tower was destroyed by the invading Jurchen forces and never remade. Su Song also wrote, collected and amalgamated other works from the era. The best know of these works are the large celestial atlas of several star maps, several terrestrial maps, works on mineralogy, zoology, botany, metallurgy and a treatise on pharmacology.

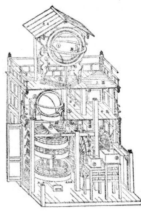

Shen Kuo

Shen Kuo, also known as Shen Gua, Cunzhong, Mengqi or Mengxi Weng was another great mind of the Song Dynasty. Often remembered as a scientist, engineer, statesman and polymath he also progressed the fields of mathematics, astronomy, meteorology, geology, entomology, anatomy, climatology, zoology, botany, pharmacology, medicine, agronomy, archaeology, ethnography, cartography, geography, geophysics, mineralogy and the encyclopedia.

He was also a military general, diplomat, hydraulic engineer, inventor, economist, academy chancellor, finance minister, governmental state inspector, philosopher, art critic, poet, and musician. He would also become the head official for the Bureau of Astronomy in the Song court and the Assistant Minister of Imperial Hospitality. Politically he aligned with Reformist faction known as the New Policies Group, in which he worked closely with the Chancellor Wang Anshi. Although the Europeans were first to employ the needle compass in the high seas, Shen Kuo is the suspected creator. His work titled *Dream Pool Essays* or *Dream Torrent Essays* first described the magnetic needle compass. In this work Shen discovered the concept of true north and magnetic declination towards the north pole. In short, his studies show how true North can be found with a suspended magnetic needle and the distance between the Pole Star. Uniquely, ancient German sundials show similar markings to this early Chinese model.

Shen Kuo and his colleague Wei Pu also planned to map the orbital paths of the Solar System over five years. Ultimately this would not be completed with massive disturbance caused in the Court and Dynasty. Before this work stopped Shen Kuo managed to improve the designs of the armillary sphere, gnomon and sighting tube. He also invented a new type of inflow water clock and devised a geological hypothesis for land formation based upon findings of inland marine fossils, knowledge of soil erosion and the deposition of silt.

Most uniquely Shen Kuo also claimed the first hypothesis of gradual climate change. Using observations he made of ancient petrified bamboos which had been preserved underground in the caves of a then dry and arid habitat, it suggested a change to the areas biome.

Shen Kuo was a prolific writer and wrote about;

x) The first drydock to repair boats suspended out of water
x) The new invention of the canal pound lock.
x) The Chinese philosopher Mozi (470–391 BC) so far is the first person in history to describe camera obscura, Shen implemented an improved version of writing and actually created a model of the camera some 2000 years later.
x) Movable type printing invented by Bi Sheng which also secured Sheng's legacy.
x) Following an old tradition in China, Shen would also create an accurate raised-relief map of the borderlands during his inspections.
x) Shen unearthed an ancient crossbow mechanism from an archaeological dig. It turned out to be a Jacob's staff, used as a surveying tool which he would write extensively about.
x) Shen Kuo wrote several other books including his most famous work, the Dream Pool Essays. Most of hist work did not survive and his poetic works only survived because of posthumous replication work. His work on the supernatural, divination, flying objects and ancient Daoist and Confucian texts were also lost to time.

Xi Jinping

Immortalized as the leader who bought China into the 21st and to some extent the 22nd century, Xi Jinping is arguably China's greatest President to date. From birth and notably adolescence Xi was interacting or involved with political figures in Beijing from the 1960's.

That was until 1969 when Xi was sent to the countryside in 1969. In this time he worked as a labourer on a communal farm. Here he developed a relationship with the local peasantry and began to understand the working class. When Xi returned to politics he rose up the ranks in the CCP rapidly. With his character, background and actual ability he became the leader of the Party and nation.

His early years as an advisor showed the flaws of the old Party and where it needed to evolve. With this motivation he moulded the Communist led state into a semi capitalist, high tech and developed nation.

Confucius

Confucianism is the philosophy of the main system of thought in China. The man, Confucius is fascinating. He held positions in government, in the dynasties and walked most of China on foot. In between advising the most powerful people of the time he also became the foundation of Chinese folklore, having authored or edited all Five of the 'Five Classics.'

He created the idea of "Do not do unto others what you do not want done to yourself" before Christianity adopted a similar principle. His legacy is that of personal and governmental morality, correctness of social relationships, justice, kindness, and sincerity, loyalty to your family, respecting your elders and ancestors while living for your cause or duty to society.

Puyi

Puyi was a man of many titles.

He was the last Emperor of China, a nominal member of the Chinese People's Political Consultative Conference and the National People's congress, an imprisoned War criminal, a Kangde Emperor and Datong. Puyi's legacy is one of Revolutions, determination, pain and non stop servitude. He was abdicated in 1912 after the Xinhai revolution and went under the radar for 5 years.

In 1917 a warlord named Zhang Xun restored the throne to the emperor. It was not until 1932 and the Japanese invasion where we see Puyi lose his throne and be installed as a puppet monarch in Manchuria. Puyi ruled this region until the end of the Sino-Japanese and Second World War. When the People's Republic of China was formed in 1949 he was sent to prison.

Puyi was the symbol of all that was wrong with the old China in the eyes of the Communist's. In short, Puyi was left to live based on Chairman Mao's decision to try and convert Puyi to Socialism. Stalin had failed to convert the last Czar of Russia to the new ideals of the nation, so if the Chinese Communist party could do so it would cement it's place as the better model. After another long imprisonment and failure to support the doctrine of the then powerful state, Punyi's health declined and he died in 1967.

Mao Zedong

If Sun Yat-Sen is the Grandfather of modern China Mao Zedong is the father. Chairman Mao was a Communist revolutionary turned founder of the nation we see today. The form of Communism held by Mao and the Government was idealogical Communism. Once implemented under Mao it recreated the first form of an independent nation in China for over 4oo years.

His theology and principles, be it political theory, policy or military strategy is known as Maoism.

Chairman Mao founded and led the following;
People's Republic of China / The Communist Party of China / The Chinese Communist Party / The Chinese Workers' and

Peasant's Red Army / The Planned economy and enforcement project agencies / Industrialisation Program / Two bombs, One Satellite Project / Sufan Movement / Anti Rightest Campaign / The Great Leap Forward / Socialist education Movement / Cultural Revolution / Jiangxi Soviet's radical Land Policy / Defeat of the Nationalist Government which withdrew to Taiwan / The Three-anti and Five-anti Campaigns / The psychological victory over Korea in the Korean War.

Sun Tzu

General, Strategist, Philosopher. Sun Tzu is perhaps the most notable military theorist of all time. The Art of War, his book and most famous creation is studied to this day by business, political and military leaders of most nations. His influence and philosophy is still shaping modern China. His strategies, guidance and rulings offer guidance on;

- ✗ Alternatives to battle and war.
- ✗ The use of spies, delays and deferring war to your advantage, or as an alternative to total war entirely.
- ✗ Making and keeping military alliances.
- ✗ Using deceit to your advantage.
- ✗ Be willing to submit to foes, either in a genuine surrender or a pretend one if it assists the bigger victory.

Deng Xiaopeng

After Chairman Mao's death Deng Xiaopeng came to power. He bought China into touch with the times. Under Deng Xiaopeng China became a modern, efficient and powerhouse of a nation. His policies resulted in modernisation and progress. He did so by reforming the ideology of Communism and Capitalism. By evolving Communism to take advantage of the rest of the worlds free markets. Control was kept by the Government but the ability to build a globally dependant market and economy were now available.

We are still seeing the results of this today. The nation and economic development are still thriving thanks to the special economic zones and initiatives he began.
Being the first of the Communist leaders coming from a land owning family he proved what a Modern Communist looked like. The vision of China and prospects of a new age of Communism took seed under his rule.

After a long career as a Party Member with many promotions and demotions it was after Chairman Mao's death that we see the first example of Deng Xiaopeng's brilliance. Mao's chosen successor was a man called Hua Guofeng and in this post Mao's China entered relative chaos. Deng Xiaopeng started and initiated a program called Bouan Fanzheng. It's goal was to restore order and it did exactly that. After the cultural revolution, the opening up and great reformation of China Deng rose to prominence in the party once again.
He started a series of political reforms including the Setting term limits for officials, the revision of China's third constitution, family planning, compulsory 9 Year education and the 863 Program for Science and Technology.
Whilst he never held the position of Head of State, Head of Government, Or General Secretary he is one of China's greatest leaders and the founder of the modern China we know.

The Members of the Central Politburo of the Communist Party of China.

The Politburo is a group of 25 Senior leaders that oversee the Communist Party of China. They have more influence, power and say than other nations senior public servants and much more privacy. The members will hold other state and party positions, with some even being regional leaders. The ruling is by consensus and the internal workings of the Politburo are not public knowledge.

The Red Guards

The Red Guards were a brutal student led paramilitary movement loyal to Chairman Mao. Their agenda was to -

"make China Maoist from inside out and then we will help the working people of other countries make the world red... And then the whole universe."

Whilst many of these students outlived this era they played a pivotal role in rapidly accelerating Communism, which is why they are in this chapter, not because anyone looks back on them fondly. Like all aggressive units or groups it splintered and fell apart from internal fighting. The core of the movement can be seen in their attacks on the 'Four Old's.' The Four Old's were the old customs, old culture, old habits and old ideas of China. During the cultural revolution the red guard destroyed much of China's history and heritage, and by doing so it allowed the old ways to be forgotten.

This was not just book burning ceremonies but countless grave robberies, public humiliation of the old ruling classes corpses and destruction of tombs, shrines, artefacts, art, scrolls, temples and much more.

A huge amount of history and knowledge was lost due to this fanaticism and something that the modern Communist nation is rebuilding.

Jack Ma

Jack Ma is the persona of success and Modern Business in China. He is an investor, founder and politician. Overlooking all of his efforts as an advocate for a market driven economy, his role as a Chinese Business Ambassador and philanthropist is known through the tech giant Alibaba. As co-founder and former executive chairman of the Alibaba Group his influence and leadership is active across modern China and the rest of the world. Despite several discrepancies with the Government (over more recent enterprises) have fundamentally been strategic, which have shown the world that the Government are still very much in control of the private sector.

Ma Huateng or Pony Ma

Ma Huateng is the founder of Tencent, now Asia's most valuable company, and if the trajectory of growth continues it will eventually become the worlds largest company. Ma's leadership saw Tencent go from startup to absolutely dominant company in Chinese mobile instant messaging, media, entertainment, payment systems, smartphones, internet services, value added services, online advertising, gaming and much more.

His influence transcends the private sector as he is also a politician and philanthropist. His character is less known than his often compared to counterpart Jack Ma. He has an investment philosophy much like the West's best investor, Warren Buffett. Choosing to back the brand, company and long term projections rather than quick or fast money.

Wang Qishan

Having served as the Vice President of The People's Republic of China, Secretary of the Central Commission for Discipline Inspection, The Communist Party's anti corruption body and member of the Politburo Standing Committee Wang Qishan is the morale backbone of Modern China.

Wang has led China into the new age with his significant contributions to the anti corruption campaigns and development of China.

Before entering politics he was Governor of the China Construction Bank, the largest bank on the planet.

His other past roles include; Vice-Governor of Guangdong, Party Secretary of Hainan, Mayor of Beijing and Vice Premier in charge of financial and commercial affairs under Wen Jiabao.

DIFFERENCES
''AS A FOREIGNER IN CHINA YOU MUST UNDERSTAND''

VI

''A man who cannot tolerate small misfortunes cannot do great things.''

差异

HOW TO DO BUSINESS IN CHINA AS A FOREIGNER

1. Bring something special to the table.
2. Ensure this special product or service benefits the society and does not offend the Government.
3. Learn the language or ensure you have a trusted and capable interpretor or bilingual associate/partner.
4. Use presentations and visual aids, Chinese culture associates certain things to certain colours, you could end up projecting the wrong meaning or purpose by accident with colours.
5. Whilst presentations are a challenging experience at first you will quickly get used to them. Your presentations should be detailed, with special emphasis on the numbers and long term benefits.
6. Only senior members of the teams talk in negotiations. You should adopt the same approach and make them known, as they will be the ones to lead the introduction and talks.
7. The fast paced yes or no meetings of the west are a long way from meetings in China. Be ready and willing to wait as decisions are never decisive and fast answered. The use of yes or no is also a rarity, for a Chinese national to say no is a huge societal grievance.
8. The slow pace has it's reasoning. Relationships are critical when doing business in China. During these long hours and days you are being assessed not only from your business angle but also your character.
9. Avoid high pressured, dramatised theatrics. Emotional blackmail or attempted manipulation will leave you out manoeuvred.
10. Be ready for hard negotiations. Decisions are hierarchical and those doing the talking will be pushing the agenda's of their seniors.
11. Your starting price should always leave room for change, be it through negotiation so they feel like they have won something.
12. There is a growing dislike for doing business with foreigners. Many Chinese businesses do not want to be dependant on foreigners or feel like they would be better without the international aspect. It is therefore your duty to be a good ambassador and fair business person. By showing you can be trusted and your intentions are reasonable it will help overcome this concern.

13. On top of this last point there has always been the 'East vs West' concept. It is not aided by immaturity on both sides, but you really must break through it in order to succeed.

14. Avoid doing business with Chinese friends if you can. Unless you are on the same side then business will strain even the most pure of friendships.

15. Never be late.

16. Learn the etiquette on presenting your business card and expect to exchange them in almost every introductory meeting. It is also wise to have one side printed English and the other in 'Simplified Chinese' if you are doing business in mainland China. If you are dealing in Taiwan or Hong Kong 'Classical Chinese' characters may be beneficial.

17. Know that most of Chinese business management is built on the foundation of Confucianism.

18. Do not interrupt the long periods of silence in meetings. Be quietly confident and dispel the image of the noisy, blabbering, money hungry foreigner.

19. Contract Law is different in China. Offer and Acceptance does not constitute a deal closed. Even if signed and agreed upon the contract is not binding and can be negotiated upon if either party has a change of mind.

19. Observe and respect the seniority. In many industries the level of seniority is more important than the actual experience or role.

20. Guilt is a tool. If you do make an error do not be surprised if you are shamed into a new avenue as a repercussion.

21. Wall street calls these tactics a few different names but they are universal and employed in China as well. 'Good cop, bad cop,' 'tensions and tempers' and 'time sensitive urgency' are all employed.

22. Clarity when it comes to a 'no deal' is difficult to come by. If the deal is to not go ahead then many Chinese business people will not tell you. It is a matter of saving face, so if they start to answer their mobile amid conversations, become stubborn, detached or inflexible they are trying to force you to back down.

WORKING IN CHINA

There are massive opportunities to be had in China right now. It is the largest economy and boasts the most potential in terms of growth and returns, if you can navigate around the political, language, culture and varying business systems. Like everywhere else in the world, graduate opportunities are fiercely competitive and workers are truly expected to work, not just show up. Saying this, everyone is entitled to work in China and if you are willing to adapt then you really can make a great life. China is producing more millionaires than anywhere else on the planet, with numbers consistently doubling.

The low cost of living, outside of central cities is phenomenal. You can get by with low rent, low food costs and near enough zero travel expenses with all the available schemes. Away from the traditional employment 'selling points' the culture of modern China is a huge attraction. The biggest factor, irrespective of professional level is language. Expat workers in China typically find jobs with foreign-invested enterprises. There is the option to work with the large Chinese companies but knowledge of Mandarin is more or less essential.

The largest industries in China are:

Chemicals - Consumer products - Food processing - Machine building - Mining – Technology – Textiles - Transport.

China is rare in the fact it is a place where almost every aspect of life and society has multiple levels. It is possible to have a dual system, a multi system and even a one way system that still operates differently on where you are and who you ask. It is important to bare that in mind as you seek employment or startup a business in China.

BEST ASPECTS TO LIFE IN MODERN CHINA

x) The level of opportunities are unmatched.
x) The food is cheap and delicious.
x) Arguably the friendliest or most curious nation on Earth.
x) The high salaries and disproportionately cheap living costs.
x) There is quality Tea everywhere.

x) China is genuinely huge and diverse, if your coming from America or Russia then the size is of the Chinese nation is on par geographically, but even more diverse.
x) China is a hub for Asia and allows easy travel around the continent.
x) Technology is a part of everyday life.
x) Big cities are safe.
x) Many of the people are gorgeous on the inside and out.
x) Be instantly popular and a local superstar. Many of the regions still have limited numbers of foreigners. Whether you have blue eyes or dark skin you will attract attention.
x) Absolute poverty has been eradicated.
x) There is no homelessness.
x) The speed at which everything adapts.
x) Everything is fast paced and constantly changing.
x) The proximity to many south East Asian paradises: Thailand, Philippines, Vietnam, Cambodia, Burma... all within, 2-4 hours by plane.

WHY ARE SO MANY PEOPLE LEAVING CHINA?

The reasons for foreigners leaving China is massively different to the main reasons for why Chinese nationals leave. Outward migration is rising while the numbers of people coming into China are yearly stable. There is massive speculation as to the why, but some common arguments are -

1. It is increasingly difficult if you have invested in China to continue and progress with Government authority and regulations. Compared to the West they are far more involved which is a bit of a culture shock, but with regulation becoming even more intertwined even on a local and micro scale, it s putting many foreigners off.

2. Education, many private schools only offer an American style diploma, when in reality the Chinese equivalent is the one needed to continue onto higher education in mainland China. In addition to this the physical cost of education in China is rising.

3. This one is controversial, and depending on who you ask it can be more of an attractant than an aspect that makes you want to leave. It

goes along the lines of the increasing government propaganda and how the nationalism can be suffocating.

4. Whilst the vast majority of Chinese nationals are fantastic when it comes to embracing people of other cultures, there is a growing anti foreign sentiment. This is a multi faced beast in itself, with regions reacting differently and even responding differently to different foreign cultures. The end result of this is small but increasingly visible. Factions of the society are becoming anti African or Anti American.

5. Within society, specifically with regard to the middle aged men of China who have seen the nation develop who want it to continue, but without or with reduced foreign investment. They are typically capitalists and nationalists, which under normal circumstances is a good thing, but now this group in particular is making it difficult for foreign investors.

6. China's foreign and own private sector involved in low level manufacturing are leaving the country for cheaper locations, like Vietnam, Cambodia and other South East Asian nations. This is for a whole host of reasons.

7. As the rest of the planet seems to be pushing the health agenda and less people taking up smoking, it is still prominent to any Chinese cities population. There is ample second hand smoke and very little concern by the actual smoker. If you have lived in China you will know more than a few chain smokers who can finish off a pack a day, and as petty as it sounds many foreigners don't like the idea of second hand smoke and the cancers that follow.

8. Perhaps the most understandable reason for the migration out of China is the pollution. It is something we all get used too quickly and quickly forget the feeling of clean, fresh air. The pull of the cities and all that they offer make us overlook the smog, dirt, grit and grime of the day to day, but the working and professional class are starting to change.

9. The lack of empathy, at least on the surface. The idea of 'face,' the history of communism and the long ingrained idea of fairly stoic principles are a party to life in China. Many millennials or individuals

165

from generation Z are not akin to this outlook and behaviour. Rather than come to understand that being 'strong and cold' on the surface and 'soft and warm' behind closed doors shows someone with a quality character, they would rather not waste their time with this crowd and return to a more opaque culture.

10. Squat Toilets.

11. Communities double standard. All that is positive about Communism is lost in many of the urban districts of modern China. You can see this in the old lady who's job is to clean the squat toilets or when you see one of the many drivers toss garbage from their car window. With the new surveillance efforts we can only hope these behaviours are eradicated and no longer a driving force for foreigners to leave.

12. There is a growing trend in the bars and small shops in China to sell counterfeit alcohol. Fake labelling, mixing in additives and a host of other practices are making people ill. Being that the brands being copied are some of the foreigners favourites it is the tourists, expats or residents getting ill the most. It is even enough to push your typical drinker over the edge and leave.

13. Like every other major city there is an inability to be physically or mentally healthy. The stress, pollution and lifestyle of these globalised hubs are too much for anyone over a sustained time. When it comes to China this is seen on an unfathomable scale, due to the sheer size of the cities.

14. The censorship is more than a simple annoyance, it has worn down many of the foreign nationals in China. Using a VPN or loophole to get around the censorship and talk to friends and family on the same platform every single time is belittling and sad. The mass internet usage and limitations are a deterrent too many young foreigners who would otherwise add value to modern Chinese society.

15. Property
Generally speaking foreigners are only allowed to own one property in China and they must live in it. Of course there are exceptions but they take time and effort. If you are thinking of coming to China and

buying a house, a business premises or a house in the countryside with land, expect a long time frame and high risk.

16. Drugs, there is no middle ground in China when it comes to narcotics. There is no sense of recreational drugs and fortunately this culture has been avoided. Whilst it is a positive, many foreigners are being drawn to this nefarious culture in weaker parts of the world and it highlights the bigger issue. When there is a rare circumstances of drug taking in China is typically hardcore drug addicts doing lethal drugs.

17. There are increasing numbers of brothels, pop up bars, illegal raves and other darker aspects of society. Whilst the odd rave may be harmless those cropping up in China are considered a detriment. These kinds of establishments can be seen on all levels of society, from the industrial hubs and centres to top tier levels of society in Shanghai and Beijing.

COMMON MISCONCEPTIONS

Misbelief, Mystery, Misconceptions and Misinformation are all rife in China. By understanding and confronting them, be it foreigners, tourists, expats, outsiders and even Chinese nationals we can begin to work on the solutions. Listed in this chapter are the most common misconceptions about the modern nation, and in no way should you take offence by any of them.

1. China is a threat. The world sees China as the biggest threat, with it's increasing military, global ambitions, strive for power across Asia and it's dominance of planet wide business. The reality is that China, or the middle income and lower households see the rest of the world as a 'non communist' threat. The movers and shakers of the nation in fact see China's global efforts as a means to build partnerships, do good business and de-escalate.
Those who don't trust China will of course question this, but without taking sides the Nine Dash Line is the most visible example of this. The Nine dash line marks the boundary of China's claimed and rightful ownership in the South China Sea.

167

China is the dominant, largest and most powerful nation in Asia and proportionately it seems logical that China should own this area of the South China Sea.
In reality we see Malaysia, Vietnam, Indonesia, Japan and the might of the United States Military encroach, build up a massive counter or defence force and question China.

2. Open anger, discontent and publicly verbal discontent with the political system means the Party is losing Power. As long as the nation continues to perform and grow the party will remain in power. As soon as stability and progress are threatened the public's open discontent or opposition efforts will increase, but not likely change the Party and it's power. China is too large and now has too many safeguards in place for the ruling party to really lose power. It is to interlinked with every aspect of the country and it's governance is critical. It may evolve as it did under the Presidencies of Deng Xiaoping and Xi Xinping but it won't be from global efforts or pressure, only internal.

3. China will become a truly open nation built on the independent character of it's people. However liberal modern China seems on the surface it never shies far from it's roots. With all the liberal efforts and agendas don't be caught out in thinking it is neo-liberal, like areas in Europe and America. Even in the hip international sections of the cities there lurks a beast of traditional and Communist opinions.
The economic efforts and open labelling in the media are not to promote individuality, free thought, increased liberalism but are a tool to bring the foreign money in, which will in turn better the rest of the nation. It is something that can be seen in many of the people too. Traditional thinking and behaviour, even with the assets of tech and infrastructure are still ingrained.

4. It is easy to find a boyfriend or girlfriend in China. For whatever reason many nationalities view the Chinese as an easy win. It one of the biggest falsehoods on the planet.
Firstly it is impossible to define a whole nation with a collective opinion and standard. Secondly the greasy idiots who think like this are fools. Like every other nation, true feelings determine the ease of the bond when it comes to a partner. The only way

this can gain some ground for the rumour is the scale of the men and ladies only interested in dating foreigners, which is of course the same for every other city or place.

5. China is polluted. There are areas in China where the pollution is dangerous and horrible, but the opinion of the whole nation being covered in smog is false. The government has and continues to counter the problem with huge initiatives. Restriction and energy programmes are rising which sees the nation become healthy once again.

6. China is packed full of people. It is true, China has a massive population, close to twenty percent of the whole planet in fact, but it is not crowded everywhere. Outside of the major cities it can actually be quite calm in terms of foot traffic and people. The balancing factor is China's scale, it has a big population but it is also a big nation so things are not as alarming as we believe.

7. Everyone in China consumes cat, dog, bats, rats, frogs and other strange cuisines. In light of the recent events the small portion of the population that eat these items are statistically decreasing. Whilst the poorest of people are forced to eat cat and but more commonly dog, (at quite staggering levels) the numbers are decreasing by 50% every ten years.

8. Chinese people within China are poor. The level of poor is different in China and whilst there is 110 million people living off two dollars a day, it is not as bad as being truly poor in the West. There is still freedom and support granted to the poor Chinese from a traditional system of Communism, which has a proven track record for allowing even the poorest to gain wealth and rise. Based on statistics the 'class system' is more in favour of people being comfortable and with little money than nearly every other nation on Earth.

9. Nobody has a vehicle. This is a huge misconception. There are at least 350 million motor vehicles in China. That is 100 million more vehicles than citizens of the United States of America.

10. Made in China means cheap and poorly made. China makes products of all levels of quality. Low, Medium and High. Whatever you are willing to pay for you can get in the modern nation.

11. All Chinese people are brainwashed and living in a regime. Whilst they may not be open about a disagreement with Government policy, or the nations part in something, it is not in Chinese culture to be loud and open about it. Even the modern Chinese nationals nature, mannerisms and behaviour is very different to the West. The repercussions for being vocal or even counter intuitive to the greater nations momentum is also very different.

12. The average citizen does not care about Government internet censorship. If the person is under fifty and not working in Government then the truth is they probably do care. The reality is that wanting and caring is very different to acting and doing. At present the average Chinese national has more going on in their lives than working toward a new standard.

13. China and the Chinese people are Godless. There are in fact several Chinese religions and people practising Christianity, Judaism and Islam. The most popular religions are Taoism, Buddhism and Confucianism – all without a God figurehead, which is where the misconception comes from.

Freedom of belief is a Government policy and practising your religion is a part of the constitution. Thirty percent of modern Chinese associate or prescribe to a belief system which is in fact higher than many other nations.

14. Chinese people have no self control. Why so many people believe this is the case is not clear. Can Chinese people be impulsive, loud and energetic at times, yes; But so can any other nationality. The scale is also so vast that there will be millions of people at both ends of the 'self control spectrum.'

15. The Police and Military are poorly trained and abuse their positions. This is one area where the rumours have no weight. The Chinese defence and security departments are disciplined, strict, loyal and comprised of men and women who have sworn their allegiance to China. The nation has the funding to support the infrastructure, defence sector and training the forces to a good standard.

16. China only copies, it does not create.

Whilst there is a huge culture and industry around copy cat, imitations, Shanzhai and replica goods it is wrong to believe that is all China does. In today's China the level of copies are going down on all levels and industries. For some reason these aspects to the society have tarnished the historical and to some extent the modern day creations of modern China.

For millennia Chinese inventors have created global products, long before globalisation. To name a few quick Chinese inventions and dispel this misconception it is easy enough.

Chinese inventions include - Paper, the mechanical clock, tea, gunpowder, compass, alcohol, silk, umbrella, kites, toothbrushes, acupuncture, iron smelting, bronze, flares, rockets, porcelain, earthquake detectors, toilet paper, Mahjong and Go board games, playing cards, seed drill, paper money, Jade-working, parachutes, fired bricks, rice cultivation, fire arrows, Soy sauce, sunglasses, Soybean cultivation, the fishing reel, incense, animal zodiac, artillery, banknotes, bellows, crossbows, dominoes, Hukou System, hot pot and many more.

The cyclical nature of the dynasties and modern age nation allowed these items to be exported and outlive the individual and society who created them. It is also easy to see a new era of Chinese creations that have been built from start to finish by Chinese companies.

17. Fortune cookies are from China. Fortune cookies were invented in the United States. You will rarely find a fortune cookie in mainland China.

18. Pudding or desert takes the form of Tea. Whilst the after meal dishes are not like puddings, cakes or sweets, and tea is drunk at the end of a meal, China has many popular deserts. These include fruit, rice rolls, sesame rolls soups, dumplings, fritters and water chestnut cake.

19. Racism in China is common. Racism exists everywhere, but in China the prejudice against some people, and not necessarily foreigners is based off culture not skin colour. If you are from a culture deemed negative to that of China or widely viewed as fanatical and destructive, there will of course be some negativity towards you.

20. All Chinese are excellent cooks. Whilst true for the past generations where the majority of people had a tendency toward creating something delicious, the younger generations are not learning how to. As tastes develop and those guarding the recipes of traditional cuisine get old and die, the current generations would rather eat out.

21. All Chinese know how to fight. Kung Fu, Karate, Wushu and other ancient fighting styles are getting rarer by the day. The time were the young men would go and practice fighting together is largely a thing of the past.

22. The population growth rate is increasing. China's massive population is in fact decreasing, albeit incrementally so.

23. Speaking English is non existent. 200 million Chinese nationals speak English and with nation wide education systems adopting English lessons the numbers are rising.

24. The Great Chinese Firewall monitors everything. It does not because it cannot. The firewall is like a wide holed fishing net, it will only catch the big fish.

25. Chinese people aren't funny. If you learn the language, and understand the Chinese sense of humour you will be laughing for hours.

26. Chinese women are submissive. Historically this might have been true, but today it could not be further from the truth. The age of bound feet is long over and the pressure on Chinese women to excel professionally is massive. Many have an aggressive sense of ambition and want to leave their mark on the world. The women of the Chinese middle class are in a better position of society than most other nations. The purchasing power, quality of life, education, culture, business opportunities and self respect is near enough unmatched amongst this massive dynamic.

27. All Chinese Are Very Smart. This misconception's originates from the culture of immigrant families in America. Education is a top priority and many families push their children to excel in academia, it does not mean all Chinese nationals are smart.

28. China is just like the movies. Whilst Chinese culture has been immortalised and translated across the world through media, it is very different in real life. In some ways the projected images should be taken with a pinch of salt, in some cases they have not portrayed the image strongly enough.

29. China's Market has grown too quickly. As the nation continues to grow it will evolve into something we have not seen before from an economic perspective. The markets will likely mature into something similar to Europe, except bigger, better and more intertwined with the international and global economy. It has grown so large that even in recessions and eras of mass trouble there is still bubbles and huge growth.

30. China will go back to it's historic role. China is harbouring change where all other nations have failed. National pride is decreasing across the rest of the world but the optimism of China's greater future is breeding a proud population. As the Government continues to stimulate new ideas and the collaboration between public and private enterprise the nation unifies. This growth and massive support is making the image and likelihood of returning to isolationism and being the factory of the world redundant.

31. The Chinese government murdered 60 million citizens. There will be many people reading this itching to say that it's a fact. The truth is that the Government cannot be blamed for their deaths or class it as murder. When 60 million people died of famine in early Communist China it was due to the disastrous mistakes and nation wide instability. It was neither deliberate or a sole consequence of the Party in power.

COMMUNICATION IN CHINA

Without giving you a language lesson the language of China is two faced. It consists of Mandarin as the most popular language and Cantonese as a close second. There are numerous sub dialects and regional languages as well.

Mandarin and Cantonese is derived from the original Sino-Tibetan languages of the past. They are not related as to correlate, but can be understandable by speakers of either one. When it comes to talking in China the tone of voice distinguishes the word being said. In some cases the same 'word' can mean up to eleven different things, all depending on the tone. When it comes to physical and non verbal communication there are several aspects unique to China. Body language will be watched and judged. When you are not acquainted with someone do not make any bodily contact. It is disliked, rude and considered far too forward.

Clicking your fingers or whistling is very rude, so is blowing your nose and returning the handkerchief in a pocket. Never gesture with one finger like the common 'come here' or point at something with a hand signal like in the West.

Over using your feet is awful when it comes to communicating. If your talking and put your feet up, or pass a heavy object with the help of your leg or feet it's frowned upon.

Facial expressions and body language relay more than confidence in China. It is all geared toward better understanding the meaning and intention of the words being said. Frowning is not just confrontational but a sign of disagreement. Therefore the vast majority of Chinese remain poker faced as you talk to them, which is a bit startling when you start out communicating. Prolonged eye contact is also rude in China. To stare at someone is almost viewed as aggressive or animalistic. Also when you talk never hold a fist as it is an obscene gesture.

INTRODUCTIONS

When you first meet someone in China the correct gesture, titles and name is considered important. When you meet people and introduce others always use Mr or Mrs (then their surname) and then their title (what they do professionally.)

When it comes to that initial meeting do not be hesitant but it is often best to watch the body language of the other person. Shaking hands is common but a nod or bow is still prominent, which you should return and emulate.

If you are meeting a group of people and it is impossible to shake hands or bow to all they may applaud you. Remain un-fazed and clap back with as much enthusiasm and smile.

The eldest or most senior person will initiate greetings. It is important that you make your introduction with them before anyone else.

When talking casually the formality of communications will often relax. Whilst jokes and chit chat is the same as the rest of the world, nuances, double entendres, puns or wordplay have been banned in China.

MANNERS AND ETIQUETTE IN CHINA

Etiquette has been in China for 5000 years. The sense of decorum and manner in which you behave is taught from a young age. Rightfully so it's ingrained into Chinese society and something we must learn more about to bridge the gap. If you are thinking you know how to behave in the West then all very well and good, modern China is entirely different. Western Etiquette is based off of decency and showing you are of a well rounded character. Traditional Chinese etiquette is about modesty and elegance. Respect is shown not through proximity, physicality or intimacy but distance.

Modern Behaviour
Modern etiquette is evolving and changing with the nation. With a growing class of 'wealthy to well off' people the resurgence in group expectations, the society and general etiquette is coming back with a vengeance.

Under the last century and high Communism the ruling party diminished societies etiquette and traditional mannerisms. Whilst creating and implementing newer variants. This remoulded form of China was of the collective and classic communist principles. Living humbly or frugally gained more respect than knowing how to behave in a certain setting, but this shift back has already started.

SEATING ETIQUETTE

Where once all people were equal there is now considerable effort to making sure people of the right class sit in the right place. Those of the high class often sit in the honourable seats, whether it be a restaurant or meeting. Those of lower class sit further away. This can be seen in any of the top schools, restaurants or clubs with private rooms and physical levels. It is also rude to sit in a seat that was not intended for you. If the host has gone to the effort to assign seats (and think about it) the best thing to do is oblige them.

There are strict guidelines, so if you are at all uncertain ask the host. Indoor seats that face East are honourable, whilst the seats facing West are not. Elders are often placed in South facing seats and the youth in North facing seats. When you are sat at the table, be sure to have your body near the table, but not too close. When you are not eating it is very important to not leave the table. Like the West, when an honoured person, or lady comes to the table it is respectful to stand. There is not a lot of difference between physical seating position on a chair. Ensure your posture is good, if you are a lady then legs together and generally just be courteous.

GIFTS

Even in modern China there is a little bit of ceremony when it comes to gift giving. A gift should be given with two hands and presented for a microcosm of a moment before collecting it.

Gifts are typically given for weddings, children being born, birthdays and Chinese New years. Do not give scissors, knives, clocks, handkerchiefs, straw sandals or flowers unless you want to end the relationship, or if it is a funeral.

If you cannot give a gift to everyone present then you should not give a gift at all. The older generations are accustomed to refusing a gift the first time it is offered. If you offer a second time they will usually accept, unless they genuinely don't want it, or deliberately choosing to refuse you. A gift in China can be offered three times before acceptance. You should never give a gift if it comes in sets of four, if the colour is black or white, or if the gift is massively valuable and you do not have an established relationship with the receiver.

Always bring a gift if you are invited to someone's home. It does not have to be grand or memorable, a bottle of alcohol, a food baskets or cake is perfect.

QUICK SOCIAL CONSIDERATIONS

x) The word 'no' is a difficult thing to say for many Chinese. So loaded questions or thinking out a conversation will help you if the request is important or tricky.

x) Older people are respected across society. Give them your seat or right of way at a door.

x) When you are applauded you should always applaud back.

x) When asked a personal question that you do not wish to answer it is best to change the subject. They will quickly understand.

x) Tipping is usually not necessary in China and it will be watched by those you dine with. Tipping should be reserved for exceptional service.

x) Chopstick etiquette is crucial. Do not stab the item on your plate or stick the chopsticks to the sky.

x) Punctuality is important. Never keep people waiting or turn up late. It is massively disrespectful and leads to tension, whatever your relations.

x) Whistling is looked upon as extremely deviant. Whistling in the day is a sing of someone up to mischief and whistling at night is for attracting the spirits.

x) Perhaps the most noticeable difference in etiquette is slurping your soup. Many a westerners will have been cuffed round the ear for slurping, in China it is a form of sending your condolences to the chef.

x) When you go to someone's house it is advisable to take your shoes off at the entrance.

x) Be ready to laugh at yourself and others. The Chinese have the ability to laugh at themselves which is pure and refreshing.

ETIQUETTE IN BUSINESS

You should never talk about business too early when conducting deals with Chinese companies or nationals. Always make time for a healthy amount of chit chat and assessment of each other pre-business. When you eventually settle down for the meeting it is best to remember Chinese Corporate Culture. Status matters. Whether it is sending the initial contact to meet an associate or a senior individual to conduct a meeting, it is important that the status is on equal levels. You should not send a low, inexperienced individual to meet a high ranking Chinese business person. It would be an insult and poor etiquette.

CORPORATE CULTURE IN CHINA

Manners and hospitality extend right up to the point of the meeting's beginning. After that it is brutal, cut throat and merciless. Below are a few advisable points to adopt or be wary of.

- English will rarely be spoken in Business meetings. It is not a lack of effort on their side. You should bring an interpreter with you or ask prior to the meeting if an interpretor will be provided.

- The highest ranking person will always enter the meeting room first. The Chinese will always assume the same with your delegation. It is the role of the most senior person to greet and make the introductions.

- Seating plays a critical role. The host will always sit to the left of the most important guest.

- It is typical for the guests to be escorted to their seats and have their counterpart (according to role or rank) sit opposite them.

- Agenda's have a special emphasis. You should send your agenda before the meeting and have your interpretor or colleague brief the host in advance. The host will also take the time to let you know their agenda.

The term 'talk a lot, say very little' is tradition and etiquette. Each member of the meeting will take their time when it is their turn to speak. It might be frustrating but often they do

179

this to convey a hidden message or test you. It is best to listen and try to understand what they are really saying.

Meetings will go from boisterous to boring and typically take a long time. Mobile phones will be ringing, conversations can be pushy and sometimes the etiquette associated to meetings seems lost on both sides.

Your should never impose your will on non deal related aspects or lose your temper. Both of these will destroy the etiquette and therefore any potential outcome. After the meeting is concluded and it is time to go for a meal you should not discuss business. Gift giving is viewed as bribery by some, so if you do give a gift make sure it is not be massively expensive. Dinner or lunches will be indirectly used to probe or gather information that will then be used in the deal or at the next meeting.

DINING ETIQUETTE

Chopsticks - Learn how to use chopsticks as they are used for all meals. When you are eating try to be polite and graceful when you take food. Never point at someone with your chopsticks and never point them to the sky or play with them. Tapping the chopsticks on the table is very rude and when you have finished eating, place them neatly on the table or chopstick rest.

Eating – When you eat you should eat quietly and eat well to show you love the food. Similar to the West you should not talk with your mouth full of food.

Hosting – If you are invited to somebody's home it is a great honour. Be grateful and bring a gift as a thank you. If you cannot make it absolutely let the host know the reason why. When you get in and take your shoes off wait to be told where to sit. Of course 'please and thank you' or offering to help is good etiquette as well.

Timing – Always be on time. When dining the next big emphasis on timing is Toasting. You should be ready to make small and frequent toasts on all occasions. The first toast is normally always after the first course by the host. The guest should then follow suite and toast after the second course. Use

180

the shot glass for toasting and generally try to avoid using the wine and beer glasses for anything other than drinking.

When you toast there is no need to empty your glass, unless the host encourages it. It is also best to toast everyone at the table before you drink as drinking alone is bad manners.

Paying – When you host someone you should pay the bill for everyone. It is also advisable to buy a dish for everyone present and then one as an extra. You should also buy a few extra plates of rice, soup, buns and noodles. The host should serve and tell the other guests to begin eating before themself.

It is impolite to leave before the guest of honour. Typically they will know that they must be the first to leave, but if they do not it is wise to carefully drop a hint about your commitments or plans post mealtime.

If you offer to host someone for breakfast it might be unusual and rare but will be met with a good reception. All the normal rules apply.

SOCIAL AND CIVILIAN OPPORTUNITIES IN CHINA

The reason for listing these civilian issues within Modern China are to show areas for potential social change or profiting through a startup. These issues are well worth reading up on before coming to China, they are in no way a political statement, just a few facts.

1. Construction is a whole different ball game in China. It is not only unfathomable as to the scale of construction projects going on but the physical process is different. It is so unlike the blue tape and licenses, permissions and rules of other nations and something that must be fully looked into. Permits, plans and projects are fast paced.

2. The environmental issues are no longer just in eyesight, they go far beyond that. Society has overcome many of the issues with smog, open landfills and a variety of other common issues we used to see.

However the new problems come from it's expansion and end cycle of goods. The strip mining practices used by partner companies, the construction projects and sheer scale of plastic waste entering the oceans from China is endangering the whole planet.

Because these issues are out of sight they are out of mind. It is the responsibility of the main cause of these issues, the Chinese middle and upper class to render support and change their consumer habits, or their future and the world will be plagued with problems.

4. Over fishing is a huge issue and Chinese companies are the cause. Chinese demand has fuelled the production and use of factory trawlers. A factory trawler is a giant ship that uses large nets to catch every species. It also uses chains to drive the fish up from the seabed or reef. These chains and nets destroy the reefs and breeding grounds, whilst killing every fish or marine species caught.

These factory trawlers then processes the giant catch on board and take them to the markets. China's demand employs more companies utilising these ocean destroying tactics than the rest of the world combined.

5. Whether you are looking at the shark fins, dog markets or any other destructive practice it is viable to come up with a social solution. Not riot or protest but to create a business that out competes the negative good. There a thousands of environmental opportunities for business ventures and startups in modern China. If you take one negative aspect and have a thought meeting with some friends, it is viable to find a profitable solution. The low level and easy practices for anyone to get started on range from collective living to vertical farming to lag grown alternatives are huge.

If you have a professional or educated background in engineering the solutions to many of China's environmental issues can be solved through business.

6. Food. When it comes to food in China nothing is small scale. Whilst vegetarianism is not widely popular there is growing predictions that many of the younger generation will transition straight to a Vegan

based diet. This transitioning of the economy and cuisine to offer products aligning with this trend offers a host of opportunities.

7. The common chopstick is also an item that presents thousands of opportunities from both a societal, environmental and business perspective. Chopstick production, specifically wooden 'one use' chopsticks are destroying the forests of China, America and Asia. The demand is such that millions of tree's are being cut to make these cheap products which, in reality are totally necessary. Many brands are offering plastic, metal and bamboo variants. All of which are re-usable and result in less environmental destruction both to create and to recycle or bin.

8. Corruption. Whilst there are still cases of corruption within regional and occasionally high levels of the public sector it is coming to an end.

9. Hygiene in many of the large cities in China can be difficult. The sheer numbers, vehicles, pollution, draining of the natural balances and scale of the urban setting destroys hygiene. Whilst most of the nation is beautifully clean and natural, there are areas (you will know them if you see them) that are a breeding ground for squalor and unhygienic standards. This of course leads to several hundred solutions to boost the society and your own business.

10. Green business. Eco business or environmental projects that add value to the natural eco-system have yet to take market share in China. This is the largest untapped civilian, social and business resource the nation has to offer. Whatever industry or field you are interested in, there is an opportunity for you. If you establish a way to setup a business that works on a green model it will quickly dominate.

CULTURE

VII

If you want to see the history go to Beijing. If you want to see the present go to Shanghai. If you want to see the future go to Shenzhen.

文化

FAMILY LIFE

If ever there was a more misconstrued image of a nations family life then it is the case of China. Chinese nationals or immigrant families will often build the image of 'Asian parents.' This stern image has been portrayed in media and in some ways become glorified, in other ways demonised. Increasingly this image of harsh parenting and pressured academia is becoming less apparent. The real truth is Chinese culture and the emphasis of a family bond (for the most part) is stronger than that of the West. As Christian family values die off and overt liberalism takes over, the importance of family life soon deteriorates. In Asia, specifically China the family unit has never been so well off, and never been so unified. The typical Chinese family has far more influence in the Children's and Grand children's life than the rest of the world, as their future is dependant on it. In some cases it is nigh on extremism, with adults being set curfews and parents inciting divorce or employing emotional manipulation to guide their Children. They only do so because they want the best for them, and this extent of proximity is rare but still visible. Perhaps this too will change as the nation becomes more Westernised, but the grandparents and great grandparents of the modern generation have one main aspiration for their children and grandchildren - To be educated and then have a better life than they did.

This is still the core of most Chinese families, whether they are above or below middle income. This idea of generational betterment was once prominent in the West but has soon be replaced with happiness. Western parents want their children to be happy, Chinese parents want their children to live a better life than they did.

The structure of Chinese families is changing as well. Traditionally the older generations of the family maintain the home, whilst those old enough to work do so, bringing money to the household. Care homes for the elderly are still a rarity in China. Those without families are often taken under the umbrella of the Socialist state, but it is the grandparents duty to look after the children, whilst the parents earn. As new found wealth gives many the means to buy more property, families are no longer all living under one roof. The issues or complexities this presents is yet to be seen.

CULTURAL HUBS

China, like all nations has culture on all levels. From the romance of the old style of living in rural villages to the truly ancient sites to the latest cultural progressions, China is arguably one of the most cultured places on Earth. The main cultural hubs are largely connected to the cuisines of the region, like much of the history, architecture and arts. The modern areas of extreme cultural interest within China are in a time of conflict. The balance between gentrification, preservation and innovation are all countering one another. Well established hubs like those listed below are well worth visiting and learning about. They are secure in their place and reputation and well worth a study or visit.

HONG KONG

Hong Kong or the "fragrant city" has a distinct cultural identity. It is the world city of Asia, where all cultures and people fuse together. Saying this the majority of the people residing in Hong Kong are ethnically Chinese, but their character is not typical of your average Chinese national. The city has shaped a distinctive off-shoot of Chinese culture and it's really something quite special. Hong Kong is where East meets West. Historically it was a trading hub and port that attracted the best of Europe and China, with some arguing this is still the case. This is most notable aspect of the culture is in the attitude of the people and the architecture. The education and mentality of the people is that of the West, where rule of law, a free economy and liberty are valued. It then has the backbone and foundation of traditional Chinese values, like family and Confucian influenced critical thinking.

History is what made Hong Kong. It's colonial influences, pace of development across all sectors and immigration levels are all contributors. The loyalty of those inhabiting this unique city is immense, with much of the population identifying as Hongkonger's and not Chinese. With this progressive attitude of the city, there is still a rare and traditional preference for a family to have boys. The role of ambitious young men is what shaped this cultural hub and it is still ingrained within the society today. When you walk the streets you will be amazed by the mix of the hustle and the tranquil. Hong Kong's nightlife is incredible, but the really special time to be alive in this city is on the summer afternoons. Whether you are visiting for business or pleasure, it is well worth learning about feng shui. This is a common and reoccurring conversation with people in Hong Kong, and China as a whole. Whether it is the layout of a friends dining room to a multi million pound construction project, feng shui will be observed and acted upon accordingly.

This cultural hub has countless sights and activities but a few of the main include;

- ✗ The Star Ferry
- ✗ Temple Street Night Market. Bazaar, Market
- ✗ Victoria Peak. Hill Station, Park
- ✗ A Symphony of Lights
- ✗ Man Mo Temple. Architectural Landmark, Historical Landmark
- ✗ Any of the markets
- ✗ Tian Tan Buddha
- ✗ Ten Thousand Buddha's Monastery
- ✗ Nathan Road
- ✗ Lan Kwai Fong
- ✗ Golden Bauhinia Square
- ✗ Wong Tai Sin Temple
- ✗ Lamma Island
- ✗ Tai Kwun Centre for Heritage and Arts
- ✗ Tai Long Wan Beach
- ✗ Afternoon Tea at The Peninsula

BEIJING

The capital of China is and will likely remain one of the most interesting places on Earth. Whatever you are interested in Beijing will accommodate. As a modern hub of not just China but the world you can find yourself in the Beijing Opera House, exploring a Ming dynasty house or heading toward the Forbidden City. Since the first Chinese Golden era to the potentially modern one, Emperors and leaders have patronized the arts, especially painting, pottery and calligraphy in Beijing. Like all capitals the objects of conquests and other beaten nations have flooded into Beijing for centuries. Due to the once hardcore communist movement evolving into it's more fluid form, these items and arts are starting to emerge. The Peking or Beijing Opera is also a whole aspect to Chinese culture in itself. The language used is not your everyday dialect and the theatrics are massively different to Western Opera.

The allegories told are more focused on the deeper meaning and morale of the story, which is likened to the much older forms of European Opera and pre Shakespearean theatre traits. In addition to restaurants there is a notable amount of teahouses, which even in ultra modern Beijing hold their market share when competing with global coffee franchises.
Some of you reading this will disagree, but the real aspect holding Beijing's place as a prominent cultural hub is not business or manufacturing, but Jingtailian or Beijing metalwork. The cloisonne metalwork, engraved gold, lacquerware combined with the thriving modern art scenes are further securing Beijing's cultural reputation. The nightlife scene is also booming, with an enormous middle class (bigger than many nations) going to events most nights. There level of events and activities to do everyday is phenomenal whether you go out to Houhai, Sanlitun or Wudakou.

Whether you live in Beijing or plan to visit then the essential visits are;

- ✗ The Imperial Palace and the Forbidden City
- ✗ The Great Wall of China
- ✗ Tiananmen Square
- ✗ Beihai Park
- ✗ The Temple of Heaven
- ✗ The Summer Palace
- ✗ Beijing National Stadium
- ✗ The Lama Temple (Yonghe)
- ✗ Beijing Capital Museum
- ✗ Beijing Ancient Observatory

CHENGDU

Chengdu, with thanks to the recent government efforts and investment bares the greatest resemblance to the ancient Chinese cities. We can only imagine the timber frames of tea houses and vibrant markets in most modern cities, but Chengdu actually has them. Chengdu is also engaged with Xiamenin, a competition as to which is the Tea capital of China (and possibly the world.) If you are reading this from Hong Kong, Beijing or Shanghai then don't let your blood boil too badly. Chengdu and it's relationship with Tea dates back at least a thousand years. The Tea Houses began with the age of the silk road and continue to this day. Historically these establishments were what pubs were to medieval Europe. They were hubs of the local community offering fragrant teas like jasmine, biluochun and longjing with beautifully ornate layouts. They were a place to play Mahjong, conduct trade or spend an evening watching the local community opera.

Chengdu is also China's party city. It competes with Shanghai and Beijing in every respect when it comes to leisure, pleasure and nightlife. Without sounding rude or derogatory, the ladies of Chengdu also have a reputation as being the most liberal and beautiful in the whole of China. Whilst beautiful people come from all over this reputation adds to the carefree lifestyle, persona and feel of the city.

Some argue that this laid back feel of Chengdu is from the cuisine and history. The home of the panda, hotpot and teahouses Chengdu, even in modern times emits a calm atmosphere, however commercialisation and development are even changing this too. Mahjong in Chengdu has taken on a whole new role, it is ingrained into the very lives of the locals. Business people, pensioners, friends, families and strangers play it every day. It is something really quite special, especially as board games around the world decline.

When you visit or move to Chengdu the places to frequent are:

- ✗ The Giant Panda Breeding Research Base (Xiongmao Jidi)
- ✗ Wenshu Monastery
- ✗ Mount Qingcheng
- ✗ Jinli Pedestrian Street
- ✗ Kuanzhai Alley
- ✗ Du Fu Cottage
- ✗ Jinsha Museum

✗ Wuhou Memorial Temple
✗ Renmin Park (People's Park)
✗ New Century Global Centre (The largest building on planet Earth.)

Chengdu is iconic in the fact that it holds the prominent aspects of Chinese culture (or the ones foreigners instantly associate with China) dearly. If you visit you will quickly find yourself in your new favourite teahouse and witnessing scenes from a slightly older and less Communist version of China.

TIBET (LHASA)

The 'third pole,' 'the place of the Gods,' 'the roof of the world' or more commonly, Tibet. It is a cultural hub and truly exciting place. Lhasa is the main city of Tibet and whilst the second largest urban area it is considered the regional capital. With an elevation exceeding 4,500 metres, the largest mountains on the planet, the third greatest volume of water stored in ice, aquifers and snow and some truly ancient sites, Tibet and Lhasa still have many hidden secrets. Lhasa was once a religious site and walled hunting ground, it is now a thriving urban area with a twist. It is one of the highest cities on the planet and traditionally beautiful. The recent influx of Han Chinese has enabled a unique culture to emerge in the present day Lhasa. You can witness both traditional Chinese culture start to mix with the native Monpa, Sherpa, Tamang, Qiang and Lhoba ethnic groups. This is creating a new age identity of the region.

Historically, and even today the UNESCO world heritage sites of The Potala Palace, Jokhang Temple, Sera Monestary and Norbulingka are essential sights to see. The mix of these two ancient cultures of Asia is effecting everything from architecture to the economy. It is interesting to witness and will either define the culture or force it to change. The political structure of the city Lhasa mirrors the physical environment. It can be deadly, isolated and old but increasingly changing. Which makes it an interesting cultural hub offering extreme sports, mountaineering, hiking and every other form of adventure.

If this is not enough of a draw for you then be warned that the romanticism of ancient Asia is still present in many areas. Whether you are interested in Buddhism or on your own pilgrimage, it is worth noting that the Monasteries will inspire you. So much so that you may even stay a little bit longer than planned, especially when the butter tea and roasted yak gets passed around.

The cultural essentials of Lhasa include;

- ✗ Exploring the Potala Palace
- ✗ Observing the pilgrims at Jokhang Temple

- ✗ Browsing Barkhor Street
- ✗ Watching or getting involved with the monks debating at Sera Monastery
- ✗ Visiting Lake Yamdrok and Lake Namtso
- ✗ Everest (Chomoluungma) climb it, clean it or just touch it
- ✗ Appreciate the real beauty of Tibetan Architecture at Tashilunpo Monastery.

TURPAN

With a special connection to Tibet the city of Turpan, Turfan or Tulufan has a long and very interesting history. It is the home of the Uyghur's, China's main Muslim population. Located in the Taklamakan desert the city has some awe inspiring features.

The ancient Uyghur people built a series of caves, now called the Bezeklik Thousand Buddha Caves between the 5th and 14th century. They excavated the desert sands and forged the tunnels and cave systems out of the hard bedrock. The caves are unique, as unlike others in China they are not the typical whole in a body of ground rock. Instead they built their homes, shrines, tunnels and likely much more in this subterranean style, both for defence and protection from the harsh conditions.

To date 77 separate cave buildings have been identified and cleaned up for people to visit, but the really interesting aspect to this culture is the timeline. The earliest cave is estimated to have been made in the 5th Century. The physical anatomy of these builders has also been bought into question. Genetically their remains are a mix of Caucasian, Indo-European and Mongoloid. This means the original culture would have been a mix of typical Indian, Chinese, Middle Eastern and European. Within the caves there are shrines to Buddha, meaning the Islamic faith was replaced at a later date. This combined with paintings and other remains show the inhabitants were travelling and trading with Ancient Persia, the Chinese Dynasties and India.

Many caves in the region are yet to be discovered and of course excavations will reveal more about this largely mysterious city and area. Turpan remained one of the unconquerable cities and regions throughout history and is supposedly home to the worlds best raisin's. The long hot summer days make for a fantastic visit, whether you are interested in the oasis's which line parts of the city, the area's history or it's unique culture.

The must stops of the city are;

- ✗ The Karez Well
- ✗ Jiaohe Ruin
- ✗ Gaochang Ruins
- ✗ Emin Minaret
- ✗ Tuyoq Village and Tuyugou Canyon
- ✗ Astana Tombs

GUANGZHOU

The most historic port city of Guangzhou plays an important role in China's history. Despite being known for it's part in the conflict between Great Britain and China, and being the only port open to foreign traders for centuries, it is now known for modern commerce and culture. The conditions of Guangzhou in the post Opium wars and then the Communist Revolution saw the deterioration of the city. It's shipping and trade fell to Hong Kong and Shanghai with ensuing city wide poverty. When under British rule this city can be used as a form of visual connotation as to the similarities between the Chinese and British. Both cultures at their core are imperialistic, proud, loyal and value tradition. Both cultures forged together through conflict in Guangzhou and even now the prosperous metropolis has these attributes.

Modern Guangzhou is famous for the Canton fair. This fair is the product, or one of the reasons behind the success of Guangzhou's industry today. Many say that Guangzhou is the best commercial city in China, and this has allowed society and culture to boom. Being central to Foshan, Dongguan, Zhongshan and Shenzhen it has taken the best of them all and become one of China's nine national central cities and an Alpha global city. It is also the most populous region on Earth and currently facing the largest inward migration in human history. Migration from Central and Southern Asia, Eastern Europe, Africa, The Middle East and Southeast Asia has given Goungzhou the title 'Capital of the third world.' This whilst looked at as a negative by many has allowed for a truly unique cultural setting. More importantly is has set the environment for some truly exciting economic opportunities. In between the massively expensive real estate markets and near dystopian mega estates you will also find the largest population of Africans in China. Guangzhou does suffer from pollution, which can only be expected from such a behemoth amount of industry and people. But the city has held 'The eight views of the Ram City' since the Song dynasty with the highest regard. The eight views of the Ram city are the eight best attractions. Throughout the centuries these have been changed according to the people and opinion of the Emperors. The full list of those included are;

Chen Clan Ancestral Hall / Temple of the Six Banyan Trees / Yuexiu Park / Canton Tower / Sun Yat-sen Memorial Hall / Nanyue King Mausuleum / Kaiping Diaulou and Villages / Museum of the Mausoleum of the Nanyue King / Yuexiu Park / Temple of the Six Banyan Trees / Sun Yat-sen Memorial

Hall / Shamian Island / Chimelong Safari Park / Pearl River / Sacred Heart Cathedral / Guangdong Museum / Baiyun Mountain (White Cloud Mountain) / Flower City Square (Huacheng Square) / Beijing Road & Shangxiajiu Pedestrian Street / Qingping Market / Whampoa Military Academy.

MACAU

Macau is the Las Vegas of China except bigger, brighter and with a better history. Culture in Macau is modern, it is a city reborn from an assortment of colonies into arguably the resort capital of the world. Macau, despite truly enormous income disparity has the fourth highest life expectancy in the world and hosts thousands of opportunities. Originally Portuguese and originally a series of islands, it is now one city. It also has separate economic and governing systems to mainland China. This has resulted in it acting as a Tax and capitalists haven of sorts, which has fuelled expansion making it the most populated area of land in terms of density. It is this intensity of people, combined with massive economic incentives that has fuelled the creation of land from what was once ocean. Two thirds of modern Macau has been created and it continues to grow. The Portuguese influence can be seen in Macau's sport, cuisine and architecture. If you speak with any local they will inevitably have some knowledge and ability to speak Portuguese or Spanish.

This combined with the unique landscape makes for a truly interesting place which is becoming more and more Chinese. Whether your walking down to the fisherman's wharf lined with super-yacht's or chasing money gambling the below are some essential places to see;

- ✗ The Ruins of St. Paul's
- ✗ Senado Square
- ✗ A-Ma Temple
- ✗ Fortaleza do Monte / Macau Museum
- ✗ The Maritime Museum and Fisherman's Wharf
- ✗ Macau Tower.
- ✗ Giant Panda Pavilion
- ✗ Guia Fortress
- ✗ Coloane Island and Hac Sa Beach
- ✗ Taipa Island and Taipa House
- ✗ Kun Iam / The Temple of the Goddess of Mercy

199

XI'AN

Xi'an descends from ancient history. It is one of the oldest human settlements and has retained it's place as a survivor by becoming a hub for trade, education, the military, cuisine, art and infrastructure. It is unapologetically Chinese in it's approach to business, development and preservation of itself. The Terracotta warriors, city wall, ancient Bell tower turned fort, turned icon and numerous museums are astounding. This combined with quick adoption of tech and having a culture of fighters, the city is quickly turning into something really special. It has been donned a city of the future for the overall atmosphere, opportunities and daily events. Being critical to defending China in the days of old and the first real city on the silk road, the city of today is treated like a national treasure in China.

Being more or less equal in distance from Shanghai and Beijing the city is a Northern powerhouse in culture as well. If you visit Xi'an beware of the mystery, low fogs and superstitions regarding the resting place of China's First Emperor and his life size terracotta army. But also be ready for the sheer amazement when you visit;

- ✗ The Bell Tower of Xi'an
- ✗ The Giant Wild Goose Pagoda
- ✗ Shaanxi History Museum
- ✗ Emperor Qinshihuang's Mausoleum site and thousands of Terracotta Warriors

XIAMEN

It is easy to see why Xiamen is labelled China's most romantic city. The long views across the ocean to distant mountains, the clean aesthetic of the buildings and palm lined beaches bring out the best in everyone. Even though it is not easily recognisable the city is still an island connected to the mainland via bridges. It has maintained this feel of 'island life' even with the high tech industry and manufacturing sectors. The ties to Fujian and Hokkien culture and relatively low pollution levels make it a place of beauty. Xiamen mixes the might of the old world from Gulangyu island with the optimism of the glass sky scrapers on the mainland.

With 10 million people visiting the now UNESCO World Heritage Site your in good company if you visit this cultural hub. Just make sure you find time to visit;

- ✗ Any of the clubs, bars or restaurants at night
- ✗ Wanshi Botanical Garden
- ✗ The beach
- ✗ Gulangyu Island
- ✗ Explore Nanputuo Temple
- ✗ Hulishan Fortress
- ✗ Fujian Tulou Clusters
- ✗ Hike the Wuyi Mountains

SHANGHAI

Traditionally Shanghai is the physical representation of where China meets the rest of the world. Now it is so much more than that. It is home to some sub cultures which have more member than some small nations. The Shanghai of old can be likened to the goods it sold, intellectual books, academic institutions, velvet and silk tailors, fishing and the first railroad were the foundations of Shanghai. Now it is the planets most forefront city when it comes to innovation of style across all sectors. Modern Shanghai is an advanced form of modern China. The old ways are still present, but slowly being forced to evolve with the greater vision of China. If you walk Shanghai at night you will see where this cultural hub is going. It is a city of the future and like a different planet. It's chrome settings, bright lights and modern aesthetic is probably the best in the world. With a population of 25 million people and a huge portion of these being young professionals, the city is destined for greatness. The buildings act as a metaphor for the projection. The infrastructure of the 1990's and 2000's was near enough primitive. Now it is ahead of every other city on the planet. Such development and growth has never been achieved in the whole of human existence. Shanghai is the city version of a catalyst for China. It shows what can be achieved for the rest of the nation; And whether you deem urbanised metropolis as a Utopia or Dystopia one thing is certain, it is going to be epic.

GUIZHOU

This difficult to pronounce region is the secret of South West China. It is iconic. The villages of Guizhou despite relative isolation at the end of the Yungui Plateau account for 35m people. There is a truly massive amount of diversity, with ethnic minorities in fact making up the majority. Guizhou borders Guangxi, Yunnan, Sichuan, Hunan and Chongqing. Whilst the rest of China has entered the 20th century and in some places surpassed it, Guizhou has not. Some would argue this was deliberate and some would say it is even a good thing. Energy and Mining make up the largest portion of this regions economy, but the real untapped resource is it's culture. The regions capital of Guiyang should be a point of call if you visit but not the main attraction. The natural beauty and 'not uncomfortable poverty' of the rural regions is the main call for a visit. This attractive landscape, whilst developing is scattered with forest, waterfalls, cave systems, rock pools and rivers. When you hear people talk about the region the words 'other wordly' continue to crop up, but the region really is the image of China portrayed in the myths and legends. The must visit sites include;

- ✗ Zhenyuan Ancient Town
- ✗ Qingyan Ancient Town
- ✗ Hongfeng Lake
- ✗ Huangguoshu Waterfall
- ✗ The Dragon Palace Cave
- ✗ Caohai Lake
- ✗ Maling River Gorge in Guizhou
- ✗ Tianxionqiao Scenic Area
- ✗ Xijiang Qianhu Miao Village
- ✗ Zhaoxing Dong village

LUOYANG

If you ever get the chance to visit Luoyang just do so, it will change your life. Luoyang will force you to question everything you ever thought about the world, including your own purpose. Louyang is in the Henan Province which explains the cuisine. It is also the region where Chinese Civilisation originated. Some of the sites here predate the known calender of human civilisation. Many of the structures and remains in Louyang are listed as being created in the 1st century, but really they predate this. From first entry to full cultural immersion the astonishing moments and discoveries of the area get greater and greater. If you overlook the manufacturing and industrial powerhouses of modern Luoyang and get to the old parts your thoughts begin to change. When you learn of the cruel baby smothering concubine turned China's first female Emperor, to the history of ancient Buddhist movements you can get a real feel for the region. Louyang was the capital of nine ancient dynasties and with the increasing amount of remains being discovered it is easy to see why.

Whether you're standing in the courtyard of the notorious Lijing gate, climbing mount Laojunshan to the Ultimate Purity Temple or boating past the Longmen Buddhist grottoes, there is one common denominator – absolute awe. These phenomenal constructions of the region were built whilst Europe, Africa, The America's and the rest of Asia were still living in the woods, caves and tribes. Luoyang was a hallmark of the Silk road and is now a hallmark of China. If you visit the below sites you will be amazed;

- ✗ Longmen Grottoes
- ✗ White Horse Temple
- ✗ Guanlin Temple
- ✗ Bai Garden
- ✗ Baiyunshan National Forest Park
- ✗ Museum of Luoyang Eastern Zhou Royal Horse and Chariot Pits
- ✗ Luoyang Museum
- ✗ Wangcheng Park
- ✗ Cockscomb Limestone Cave
  The National Peony Garden

SUZHOU

If you can imagine waterfront pagodas, canals and indisputable beauty then you can come near to imagining Suzhou. Suzhou is China's equivalent to Venice, except double the age and equally as beautiful. With it's proximity to Shanghai the influence of new age buildings and China's ambition for nation wide industry has set aground here as well. This influx of modern business has bought wealth and arguably gentrification, but it has also put Suzhou on the map. Through this industrialisation Suzhou has become one of the fastest growing cities on the planet and it is not likely to slow down. Located on the Yangtze River and Lake Tai it mixes nature, old world culture and aesthetic with modern ambition. When you find yourself in a traditional restaurant two feet from a jade coloured canal be sure to take a look at the skyline. It is in these moments where you can really take in the beauty and unmatched atmosphere of Suzhou. With it's outward expansion, land creation efforts and crazy glass skyscraper district the cultural significance of this hub will only increase. A few essential visits for your time here include;

- ✗ Humble Administrators Garden
- ✗ Classical Gardens of Suzhou
- ✗ Any of the canal side teahouses or restaurants

HUANGSHAN

Huangshan is the embodiment of ancient China in a natural form. It is an essential site for the Modern nation it terms of spirit, inspiration and legacy.

If you have ever seen a classical Chinese painting of mountains then chances are it's of Huangshan. Huangshan's literal translation is Yellow Mountain. Huangshan is the name of a mountain range and region sporting some of the most surreal sights on planet Earth. The mountains are near vertical with trees latched to the rock faces of up to 1800m. Whilst being in Eastern China it is probably the furthest image from concrete mega cities, cars and sky scrapers imaginable. The hot springs, hiking trails, temples or allure of the scenic waterfront city and it's famous bridges will stay in your memory for years to come. Huangshan helped to mould all Chinese culture, art, literature and folklore. It is as much a cultural hub as it is represented as 'the culture' of Ancient times.

Significance of Chinese Cultural Hubs

Hu Jintao said 'The Chinese culture belongs not only to the Chinese but the rest of the world.' This former leaders effort was paramount to the development of the nation and opening it to the rest of the world.

The cultural hubs listed are valuable and very much fit under his statement. Whether you are Chinese or not these sites, among the many others not listed, are a part of our species history and well worth learning about for a greater understanding.

SOCIAL RELATIONS IN CHINA

The city, the nature, the industry, the physical geography and political system all determine how the local society thinks, behaves and responds to each other in China. Modern China is simply too vast and too diverse to say this part of a certain culture acts like this and the new culture acts like this.

There is an enormous amount of crossover in terms of social relations, but there are some pivotal aspects to understand even as the nation liberalises. The Chinese nationals who lived through Mao are traditional and what many in the West would class as stern but polite. They continue to uphold a strong sense of decorum and pride. Many, even today believe in the Communist motto "Serve the People."

Rich or poor this older generation are for the most part decent and family centric. Historically the older generations have stayed in the family home to help with children or day to day activities. There is also a strong sense of 'respect you elders' across the whole spectrum of society which pairs with the other ideal of familial networks. The concept of viewing and calling a close friend of the family, your friends parents or your parents friends uncle or auntie is prominent.

It verbally sets a sense of proximity, trust and love for the individual and it's fantastic. The parental influences and idea of being a role model is installed with this practice and forces responsibility and harbouring and moulding decent youth. Outside of the close networks of family circles or old time friends there is another aspect that is different to the rest of the world. The Confucian school of thought that everyone has a place in society. This has survived and is still easily witnessed across China. It allows individuals to exhibit their talents or skills and network or build friendships with those on the same level.

This gained massive weight in the classless society of old school communism, but it has evolved with the current nation. Very broadly speaking friends are often in the same socio economic background, and very commonly the same professional field. Also among modern China the term face continues to grow in importance, even amongst social relations.

SHIFU AND KOWTOW

Shifu translates to 'skilled person,' 'master' or 'teacher.' Within modern China there is still a huge respect given and commanded by masters of their field or expertise. This respect transpires beyond those working directly or even in the same industry as 'the shifu.' If an individual has devoted their life to becoming the best or to a world standard at something, be it cooking or accounting, the modern and traditional Chinese alike comprehend and value it.

The Kow Tow, or deep bowing of you upper torso, or even to the point of getting on your knees is the highest form of paying respect across Eastern Asia. It is typical of the 'old school Chinese' that believed in self worth and not collective self worth. Whilst the act is decreasing it is worth employing in places of worship, when meeting elders, people you deeply respect and amongst your spouses parents, if they initiate it. This physical act of bowing and lowering your head is misinterpreted by many across the rest of the world. By doing it you are forced to humble yourself, which with the ego's of many alive today is not an option. It is also largely seen as a submissive act which is further from the truth. Inflated self worth, collective misunderstanding and narrow mindedness is the reason why the rest of the world lost respect for their own 'Shifu's.' Fortunately it remains a core aspect to social relations and society as a whole in modern China.

RED ENVELOPES

If you are from a Chinese or South East Asian family then you know what a red envelope is. To those that have no clue it is a monetary gift given on special occasions. It comes in an ornate red packet or envelope and is typical at every birthday, graduation, wedding or child's birth. Anyone can give a red envelope and it is a nice custom to adopt which proves your character and intentions.

DATING IN MODERN CHINA

What was once quite a conservative topic in China, talking about and actually getting involved in the dating scene has normalised. Whilst it depends on so many different influences or variables and the individuals character or preferences, dating in China can be enjoyed if you understand a few aspects;

Locations

As China enters a new cultural golden age it is ideal and worth taking advantage of. Making a day out of the museums, art galleries, tea houses or newer districts will go down well. Whilst going for a drink in the evening or coffee in the day is growing in popularity, taking your date to a boutique pop up restaurant, or even exploring the street vendors allows for a really enjoyable and 'non awkward' time. Group dating is a thing, it is casual, not so intense and if you have a good bunch of friends or network you will inevitably meet someone good. The park might be tricky but the act of taking your date for a long walk somewhere natural is a great way to build a rapport and learn about each other. It is also nice as it allows both of you to go and talk about it with your friends and family. This can either cement or dismiss some of your initial feelings. The best bit about modern China is the sheer variety and scale of the society. There are events going on every single evening so you won't ever be pushed to find something. A trip to the farmers market (with attempted haggling) and follow up meal is a guaranteed impressionable first date anywhere. In modern China it could even turn out to be a memory you cherish. With a strong book industry it is also a great idea to learn about your dates psyche if you both go to an open book reading. Between listening to the storylines and content it will give you both something to talk about, and please do feel free to share your opinion of this book!

As trust builds the dates can turn to adventures and allow you to go further afield. The options for romantic and exciting trips are almost second to none and it terms of cost it's fantastic.

Who pays?

The trend in modern China is to split the bill. If the individuals are from the middle class the one who pays is viewed as the dominant individual, hence why many (especially the young professional ladies) refuse it; But deep down it is fair to say we all know it is the gentleman's place or the person who asked the other out to pay, and it will do you justice.

Sidenote - If you are dating in China today at some point you will hear the rumours. For some reason the ideal of a traditional Chinese family pushing for a partner of greater or equal socio-economic status has been blown out of proportion. Don't take this to heart as if it is the case you will quickly see through it... and don't forget – true love conquers all.

Activities

Location, chemistry and interests are all important when it comes to dating, especially in China but a lot of emphasis is on the actual activity. Whether you are an expat or returning to China, a good activity will de-escalate any nerves or pressure, especially if you do quite like your date. Whether you care about it or not the aspects of profession, commitments, schedules and the rest all play a part. The most notable of this dating trait in China couple's doing things they would normally do alone with one another. We are not talking about things like eating or showering but more normal things, and these then take on the aspect of a date. For instance when in university a date can and does take the form of studying together, which translates to bonding and makes the academic process enjoyable.

This also translates into people doing business together or whatever mutual aspect both parties are involved with at the time. It is not uncommon for the rural Chinese to often go fruit picking, fishing or spend the day harvesting together. Which is actually quite beautiful.

Pressures and problems of Dating in Modern China
With such a vast amount of people you would have thought the pressures and problems of dating would be minimal. They are not catastrophic but worth bearing in mind. The former Governments one child policy increased the already disproportionate but natural sex ratio. Without going into the history of it, from a dating perspective it resulted in a nation with a dating deficit. The adult generation living in this time were sadly subject to a numbers game, which was not in the favour of many millions of men. With thanks to the evolution of the nation, efforts of the Government and leadership we see the balance restored. Nature and effort has eased match making across the nation, which is still subject to a few unique cultural pressures.

The Chinese family is built on commitment, so it is not unusual for those trying to join it, or date a member of the family to be tested. Predominantly this testing comes from the parents trying to judge the character and incentive for their child's partner. It is a fantastic way to fortify relationships but in the eyes of the modern youth a bit too involved.

The one area where this conscious attribute becomes extreme is in daughters about to enter higher education. In this case an abnormal amount of effort will be made by the parents to shun any and all relationships and dating. This is unless they graduate and are from a traditional background. If this is the case many parents will organise dates and introductions. Some parts of this is charming and works, but it is increasingly becoming a frustration.

On November 11th there is an annual Holiday called National Singles Day. Across the whole of China if your single there will be some form of pressure to go out on a date, even if it is just the elderly neighbour asking what you have organised. Many have warm feelings towards this holiday and even a few counter cultures have emerged. There is also a decreasing number of Chinese nationals dating and marrying foreigners. Perhaps this is just a random fact or perhaps it highlights a growing trend in China. As other nations open their borders and allow easy nationalisation or citizenship through marriage, China has rightfully kept a firm grasp on it's backdoor or loophole migration. The policies are far more sensible than a lot of the West and ensure that a person is not just marrying for a new passport.

Young Chinese nationals are also not getting married for a whole host of reasons, ranging from money, to career goals to simply not believing in it.

CULTURAL TABOOS

✗   Don't whistle at night – it attracts ghosts.

✗   Don't share a Pear.

✗   Use Chopsticks correctly.

✗   Don't wear green hats.

✗   Don't cut your hair in the first month of the lunar year.

✗   Don't cry on New Year's day.

✗   Don't give someone white flowers.

✗   Don't give a clocks as a gift.

✗   Don't split the bill at dinner.

✗   Try to avoid the number 4. It is associated with death.

✗   According to Chinese tradition, good things come in pairs. Therefore odd numbers are avoided for birthday celebrations and weddings.

✗   To avoid bad things happening in pairs, activities such as burials and gift-giving are not performed on even-numbered days.

✗   Shopkeepers sometimes refuse to read books at work because "book" (書, shū) sounds like "lose" (輸,shū). Essentially they fear it will mean a loss in the business.

- ✗ When it comes to sweeping, shopkeepers are careful not to sweep toward the door, especially during the Chinese New Year, in case good fortune is swept out into the street.
- ✗ When eating a meal, never turn over fish when you are with a fisherman as the motion symbolizes a boat capsizing.
- ✗ Never offer a friend an umbrella or scissors because they are associated with cutting ties or never seeing one another again.
- ✗ Hungry Ghost Festival - Held during the seventh lunar month you will see the effects of this festival across society. Celebrations such as weddings are not held, fishermen do not launch new boats, and many people opt to postpone their trips in this month. To avoid seeing ghosts people will also avoid going out at night.
- ✗ On your Birthday it is custom to slurp a long noodle and not bite or cut it. If you do so it is believed to shorten one's life.

THE CHANGE IN CHINA

CHINA

VIII

"The best time to plant a tree was 20 years ago. The second best
time is today."

THE CHANGING 'FACE' IN CHINA

The true test of someone's character is how they act when they are down, not when things are going in their favour. The exact same applies to nations. China is facing mass unemployment, a trade war, the repercussions of Covid, war in the cybersphere, growing commercial tensions and heated international relations. Of these there is only one aspect that could do a great deal of harm to China and that is regarding the Covid Outbreak. If it is true that some information has been hidden, or efforts were made to protect other areas in China and not the world community or that China has been trading and buying in markets strategically it would spark mass anti - China sentiment and politics.

The DNA of China is cyclical, its power, its era's and it's growth have always run in cycles. For whatever reason this be, the cycle is now at a level where a large drop in the system, economy and structure is unlikely. The 'bottom line' of the nation, or where it could go in a worst case scenario is still higher than when it has peaked in the past. This is the mental state needed for China to heal. Modern China is prominent in the structure of the world today and even with it's 'face' changing internally it is getting easier to understand. If the ruling party continue to refine policies and adapt to the thought of the modern people, then the future of China is secure.

THE CHANGING IDEALS

Chinese culture has undergone a silent revolution in the past few years. This surpasses the revolutions of the past, based purely on the fact there have been no direct casualties or actual opposition. The demand for old Chinese and modern foreign ideals and etiquette is just one of many illustrations for an even greater change taking place. Etiquette is the most visible aspect of the new class system in China. The class system is second to the Government but growing in prominence with the daily increase in millionaires and billionaires. Wealth creation in China has exceeded America and every other free and capitalist state. The market and opportunities available for international, as well as internal Chinese based business is unmatched.

The system is such that these individuals who are making a lot of money and adding value to the society are beginning to change the ideals of modern China. This transcends beyond consumer goods and lofty goals and goes right into behaviour, expectations and decorum of the working class.

IDEALS OF LIFE AND LIVING

It would be fair to say that the average Chinese national will want two things, the first being peace and the second being to enjoy their life. To achieve both in China you don't necessarily need a great deal of money. So for the majority, people's greed and desire for excess is actually quite small on a personal level. The reality is that the scale and segments in China are now so vast that even the proportionate sector of economically driven individuals is in the millions.

It is this group of middle income to very wealthy people that are driving the change in ideals and culture. Every major city is westernising and that is easy to see with the designer outlets and growing numbers of foreigners. The recent visible change is in the top end of this segment of society, the ones who are educated in top universities, sent to finishing schools overseas and adopting classic Western habits and hobbies.

These moulding of ideals can be seen in the Polo, Racing, Yacht and private members clubs popping up all over China. It is quite phenomenal to see how these pursuits and behavioural patterns are merging with the neo-traditional Chinese ways. The idea of a home, or homestead is also increasingly desired by middle income families. This idea of open hospitality, with a big garden, patio and guest bedrooms is peaking in China.

Home living, especially in light of the 'work from home' and quarantines of covid-19 are further cementing this dream. The desire for home living, with friends and family nearby is growing and as the Chinese nationals own wealth grows it is becoming a reality.

WORRIES AND BURDENS IN MODERN CHINA

Whether you are a citizen or a visitor these are some of the aspects the people and nation are concerned with and trying to overcome.

✗   National pride is swelling.

There is nothing wrong with being a patriot and proud of your home. But when it comes to a stage where some people feel threatened it might be good to reassess.

✗ People

Like everywhere people are always different and at first difficult. Once you understand someone you can then build a rapport. The issue here is the whole face of the nation is changing so quickly it becomes very difficult to get a grasp or understand them.

✗ Communication

The rest of the world communicates in such a different manner to the Chinese that it is a cause for much tension. It is very much a burden on most people, especially if they are impatient and not willing to understand one another – this applies to both side.

✗ Rumours

There has never been a time or nation on Earth that has so many rumours about it and within it. Rumours in China are prominent and cause so much unnecessary stress.

✗ Misinformation

Like rumours the sheer amount of information that is not true is astounding. The info wars are also prolific and the control of information even more notable.

✗ Fear mongering

This may sound like an overwhelming and massively generalist thing to read, but the majority of people in China are defensive. Fears about real and made up threats are so common it is in fact a little sad. For whatever reason fear and fear mongering is prevalent and only getting worse in much of the nation.

✗ What can I actually talk about?

If you are in mainland China it is still important to control what you talk about and more importantly what you do. If you are anti government in anyway, you will very quickly find yourself in big trouble.

When it comes to talking of course be honest and be sure to support the Government, their policies and their actions, as for the most part they are good. What you should not do is talk about -

- ✗ Human Rights
- ✗ Anti state anything
- ✗ Challenge its power
- ✗ Intellectual Property
- ✗ Taiwan
- ✗ Hong Kong
- ✗ Tibet
- ✗ 9 dot-dash line
- ✗ Xinxiang
- ✗ One child policy
- ✗ Controversies
- ✗ Ouiga Muslim re-education camps
- ✗ Tiananmen Square
- ✗ Handling of the outbreak in Wuhan and the Coronavirus outbreak origin/conspiracies

- ✗ Emissions and pollution

Both emissions and pollution are gradually decreasing in China, but it is still a valid cause for concern.

- ✗ Becoming a Surveillance state

Many, many people voice their concerns and fears about the use of surveillance in the cities. Essentially it is only bad if you are up to no good, or if someone manages to abuse it.

- ✗ The macro scale of everything.

The good, the bad, the ugly, the beautiful. They are all present in China and on the biggest scale of human existence. When the problems are bad they are massive, but it is proportionate. It is a worry as both the mass markets and the niche activities are all on a scale that is now noticeable.

- ✗ Cyclical

It is no secret that China's history has followed a cycle of peaking and troughing. The real question is will this strange curse and cycle be lifted with modern China, or will it be a genuine and realistic worry and burden in the future.

REASONING

By addressing these issues it becomes easier to understand them. Many Chinese people do fret and are concerned about some things to the point of paranoia. The reasoning for the above issues is down to one main thing. The nation is young. Whilst all modern world powers are centuries old the China of today is still younger than many people reading this. To put it in human terms it is like the nation, despite now being the most prominent nation on the planet, has not even reached adolescence. This can put most of us at ease knowing that these issues are still relatively small compared to the issues of other nations, when at the same time frame of their existence. We must all remember that there are dips and curves to every trajectory. The worries, burdens, legitimate concerns and actual problems in China are not terminal.

CHINA BY THE YEAR 2049

The year 2049 is a significant milestone for China. It marks the one hundredth birthday of the Peoples Republic and the realisation of the Chinese Dream, via the goals set in the Two Centenaries.

The goals and concept was first discussed at the 15th Party Congress held in 1997. Whilst it remained a topic for discussion very little was acted upon until Xi Jinping became General Secretary. In 2012 at the 18th National Congress of the Communist Party of China President Xi Jinping set the goals for each of the two 100-year anniversaries.

By 2021 a Xiaokang society will have been achieved. Xiaokang means to be moderately well off and is the outcome of a pedigree socialist and Confucian theory. A more quantitative understanding is the nation will have roughly doubled it's per capita income figures from 2010. This stage will also mark the centenary year of the Communist Party of China.

By 2049 the centenary of the founding of the People's Republic of China will be realised. By this year China will have evolved to become a strong, democratic, civilized, harmonious, and modern socialist country.

221

By 2149 China will have taken over the world... only joking. The plans for this year are known only by the senior leaders of the Party. But chances are, if your reading this you and I will likely dead, so what does it matter.

GREATEST THREATS TO CHINA

x) Xi's departure from office and the legitimacy of Communist rule after Xi Jinping retires.

x) Whether the rate of growth and trajectory of China's goals are met or missed.

x) To see if modern China can avoid the same cyclical nature as every past dynasty and national structure.

x) Increased collisions with America in territory, trade, influence and global affairs.

x) How the world holds China accountable for COVID 19.

x) Environmental devastation via demand. Seafood, woodland and the entire nation of all wanting and buying cars, precious metals/stones/non-sustainable products etc.

x) Competition with South East Asia in the manufacturing sector.

x) Road safety.

FAITH IN CHINA

Overall the forecast for China is positive. The progress taking place each day continues to set new records for world history. Whilst the same can be said for the less positive aspects, like demand for natural resources and unsustainable development, the policies being set in motion today will negate some of the damage.

Globally faith in China is increasing as the nation liberalises and becomes more open. Many nations will hold China in a negative light out of principle or cultural opposition, but most of the world sees the Chinese people as friends.

There is some hesitation to say the same for the Government, as the mid level echelons are still corruptible. The leading influencers of China present their plans openly and despite being shrouded in privacy, are fairly opaque. The faith in them and the evolving

Communist system is growing too. The hardships and problems of the past have been overcome and the new model is creating a national system which proves massively successful.

When it comes to faith in China it is best to remember the words of Confucius – "A man who chases two rabbits catches neither." Will the nation seek to follow the West in drastic liberty, fairly centralised capitalism and a different kind of freedom (which allows for personal gain), or will China continue to mould a new age Communist society? The answer will be decided by those alive today and the outcome will dictate the planets future.

Stories from the Ancient Silk Road and Great Wall

THE STONECUTTER WHO WAS NEVER SATISFIED

On a hot summer day in ancient China, a stonecutter worked long and hard swinging his hammer under the blazing sun. As he wiped the sweat from his brow, he thought to himself, "Surely the sun is the most powerful being in the world. I wish I could be the sun!" he cried.

A fairy heard his wish and the sun he became. Without wasting a second, he began to send hot sunbeams down to the land. It was wonderful to shine so bright! Then a cloud came drifting along and his light grew dim. How could that be? A cloud mightier than him! Now a white, fluffy cloud was what he wanted to be. That wish too was granted and he became a cloud, happy just to float through the blue Chinese sky.

Then along came the wind. It fluttered and whirled around him and would not let him be. "If I can't have my peace, then I'd rather blow free," he declared. "I want to be a fierce wind!" The fairy listened and once more she offered help. Now he twisted and twirled. He teased branches and chased leaves. He dashed here and there, until he blew against a rock that stood in his way. He blew as hard as he could, but the stone didn't move. "If I were a stone," he thought, "no one would bother me. A stone is the best thing to be!" So the fairy turned him into a big, heavy rock.

He sat very still and watched time go by. Until one day a group of stonecutters came his way. They pounded away at him – just doing their job. "Please, fairy!" he begged. "Being a stone is not what I want after all. From now on I want to be nobody else but me." One last time, the stonecutter got his wish. He picked up his hammer and went back to work under the sweltering sun.

THE GOOSE WHICH LAID GOLDEN EGGS

This Greek story is one of Aesop's fables and was told in many lands along the Silk Road. The scenes shown here are based on a mural illustrating the tale, found near Samarkand in the ruins of a merchant's home. There once was a man who owned a wonderful goose. Every morning, the goose laid for him a big beautiful egg – an egg made of pure, shiny, solid gold.

Every morning, the man collected the golden eggs. And little by little, egg by egg, he began to grow rich. But the man wanted more. "My goose has all those golden eggs inside her," he kept thinking. "Why not get them all at once?" One day he couldn't wait any longer. He grabbed the goose and killed her. But there were no eggs inside her! "Why did I do that?" the man cried. "Now there will be no more golden eggs."

THE LION AND THE HARE

This tale appears in an ancient Indian book of stories from the time of the Silk Road, the book became very popular in the Middle East after it was translated into Persian, Arabic, and Hebrew. In ancient times, a ferocious lion lived in the forest, killing without remorse. The other animals were terrified. To stop the lion's deadly hunts, some animals offered to provide him with food each day. Some animals would still die, of course, but the rest would live in peace. The lion agreed and enjoyed months of the easy life.

One day it was the hare's turn to present himself to the lion. Although small, the hare was very crafty. "Lion, lion," the hare cried out as he approached. "Help me, help me! Another lion is trying to eat me. But I am to be your dinner! You must stop him!" Furious that someone was trying to steal his food, the lion demanded, "Take me to the thief. I will make him pay for this mischief!" The hare and the lion made their way through the forest, eventually reached a deep well. There the lion looked down and saw his own reflection in the water.

Thinking he had found the creature who tried to steal his food, the lion jumped down, ready to fight. Alas, the lion never came out of that well, and the animals lived in peace from that day on.

THE WIDOW'S TOWER

At the Tai Ping Zhai section of the Great Wall near Huang Ya Guan, there is a well-known tower called the Widows' Tower. It is said that when building Huang Ya Guan, 12 soldiers from Henan Province lost their lives. Their wives, upon learning the news, were all heart-broken. Later, they used the compensation they got to build the tower in memory of their husbands.

THE TEN BROTHERS

People look at the Great Wall of China with admiration, but the sufferings of the people in ancient times were not appreciated at all. In fact, people were angry of all these unfair forced labour. People suffered and endured all the time. They had to fight the harsh climate, the continual attacks from Xiongnu, one of the tribes to the North of China. People died while building the wall and more people still came to build it.

Once upon a time, there were ten special brothers. The eldest can hear voices from a long distance, the second could see objects a thousand lis (500km) away, the third had the strength of an ox, the fourth had a head as hard as steel, the fifth had a body as hard as steel, the sixth had very long legs, the seventh had a very huge head, the eighth had extremely large feet, the ninth had a large mouth while the tenth had enormous eyes big enough to scare everybody.

When they were working on the farm one day, the eldest brother heard somebody crying. The second brother took a look and found out that the Great Wall builders were crying because of hunger. The third brother grew anxious and angry and immediately went to the place to help. When the officials saw him coming, did not bother to ask who he was and to what purpose he came for, they decided to chop off his head. The second brother saw this on the farm and informed his brothers. The fourth brother rushed to the rescue.

The officials chopped his head with all their might in vain. They then came to the decision of beating his body. The fifth brother came to the rescue and the officials tried once again in vain. They then wanted to throw him into the sea. The sixth brother arrived just in time and stood easily and comfortably in the sea. He caught about thirty kilograms of fishes by the way. The seventh brother then came and used his hat to take the fishes.

The eighth brother went to the mountain to chop some firewood to cook the fishes. The ninth brother devoured the fishes in one mouthful. The tenth brother became angry and cried. His tears then made a flood and left part of the Great Wall in ruins.

WANGXIAO TEMPLE

Once upon a time, there was a young boy of twelve years old. He had special abilities in his strength. He was still young but could exceed the strength of a normal grown-up. His name was Wangxiao. At that point of time, the construction of the Great Wall had started. Strong males were forced to unpaid labour along the Great Wall. Wangxiao could not escape it.

He was still naïve and did not comprehend much of the human world. During his day works, his fellow workers who were all grown-ups, took advantage of his youth. They let him do the works for them while they could relax a little bit. Wangxiao did as he was told to willingly. Unfortunately, he was still a small kid. He died soon because of overworking. People took pity on him after that and built a temple for him so as to remember him and named the temple, Wangxiao Temple. It is very near to the Great Wall.

Yanmen Fortress

Yanmen fortress, or the Wild Goose Fortress, is an essential part of the defense of the Great Wall of China. It was formerly called the Xijing Fortress. There is a story of why the name was changed as recorded here.

There was a monk who was then travelling around the world to help himself in his studies of Buddhism. He came by the fortress one day and felt quite hungry. Nobody lived around the place and therefore, he could not get any food from the local people. Some wild geese were flying pass him in the sky. He looked up and saw not only the geese but also the meat. He was lured. However, it is a big offence to kill a living creature and consume the meat for a monk. The idea simply flashed past his mind and he apparently did not take much notice of it. Unfortunately, one of the wild geese knew this and sacrificed himself for the monk. He dropped to the ground right in front of the monk and died on the spot.

The monk was amazed. When he realized that the wild goose had taken his own life to satisfy his hunger, he was touched. He could not eat the goose, not only because of the seriousness of the offence and his determination of following the Buddha instead of giving up half way, but also because of his respect to the goose for self-sacrifice. He buried the goose and built a small pagoda beside the grave.

Special Custom Along Jiayu Fortress

Jiayu Fortress is the Western end of the Great Wall of China. It is a huge fortress that marks the end and the beginning of the Great Wall. Beyond it, lay the barren Gobi desert in which nobody lived. Only travellers and traders risked their lives in passing the great fortress and their lives depended on destiny. In ancient China, and perhaps in present day also, people had the habit of testing their luck which they believed would predict the outcome of their travels.

Travellers and traders had the custom of throwing stones on the walls of the Jiayu Fortress. If the stone created noise, no matter loud or not, it would be a good sign that they would at least be safe out of the fortress. On the other hand, if no noise came about, they would probably be lost in the vast unknown world and should never return. If the sign is good, they might make a fortune and most importantly, return safe and sound. If the sign is a bad one, they might be hindered of their decision of venturing out. Such habit existed along the Jiayu Fortress.

Metal Soup Great Wall

About 60 km north of downtown Beijing there is a famous section of the Great Wall called Huang Hua Cheng (the yellow flower fortress). During summer, the whole area would be colored by yellow flowers, hence the name Huanghuacheng Great Wall (Yellow Flower Great Wall). There is a story behind the building of Huanghuacheng Great Wall.

Its construction began in 1575, during the Ming Dynasty and General Cai Kai was in charge of the entire works. It was said that it took many years to finish the construction. When General Cai Kai went to the capital and reported to the emperor his successful task, he was put to death at once!

229

Some jealous ministers had told Emperor Wanli at that time that the General Cai Kai had spent too much money and the construction of the wall was poor. The emperor was so unhappy with these false reports, he ordered Cai's immediate execution. Later the emperor sent a trusted aid to check Cai's Wall.

The aid went back and reported to the emperor that Huanghuaheng Great Wall was solid with the finest workmanship. Sorry for his hasty in putting the death to Cai, Wanli sent people to build a tomb and memorial stele in memory of the loyal general. The Emperor Wanli also wrote the two characters "Jin Tang" (Metal Soup) , meaning "solid and firm", carved on the face of a huge rock below the wall, showing the wall was firm and solid. So the wall is sometimes called Jintang Great Wall.

The Xifeng Kou, or the Happy Meeting Fortress

There is a fortress on the Great Wall originally named, the Xifeng Kou, or the Happy Meeting Fortress. There is story of how the name of the fortress came about. The Great Wall required soldiers to be on guard at the place all year round. Not only the soldiers suffered from this, their family members did not have a good time, too. Once, a young soldier had gone to defend the northern territory of China along the Great Wall for many years.

The army prohibited anybody from leaving his duty. The young man had a father as his only family member. The father was old and feared that he might not see his son ever again. Therefore, he set forth on the visit to the Great Wall in order to see his son for perhaps, the last time. When he came to a fortress, he accidentally met his son whom had grown up. His son, too, recognized his father. The two family members greeted each other with embraces. They laughed out of joy and they cried out of grief. To everybody's surprise, they both died on the spot.

In order to remember the loving father and son, the name of the fortress where they met was named Xifeng Kou. They represented the heart of thousands of soldiers and their family. The pass where they were buried was later named Xifeng Kou Pass.

THE LEGEND OF THE BEACON TOWER

In addition to the above-mentioned stories about the construction of the Great Wall, there are also plenty of stories about current scenic spots. A famous one is the legend of the Beacon Tower. This story happened during the Western Zhou Dynasty (11th century BC-711 BC). King You had a queen named Bao Si, who was very pretty. King You liked her very much, however Bao Si never smiled. An official gave a suggestion that setting the beacon tower on fire would frighten the King's subjects, and might make the queen smile. King You liked the idea. The subjects were fooled and Bao Si smiled at the sight of the chaos. Later enemies invaded Western Zhou, King You set the beacon tower on fire to ask for help. No subjects came to help because they had been fooled once before. Thus, King Zhou was killed by the enemy and Western Zhou came to an end.

The Legend of Jiayuguan Pass

Another legend about the Jiayuguan Pass tells of a workman named Yi Kaizhan in the Ming Dynasty (1368BC-1644BC) who was proficient in arithmetic. He calculated that it would need 99,999 bricks to build the Jiayuguan Pass. The supervisor did not believe him and said if they miscalculated by even one brick, then all the workmen would be punished to do hard work for three years. After the completion of the project, one brick was left behind the Xiwong city gate. The supervisor was happy at the sight of the brick and ready to punish them. However Yi Kaizhan said with deliberation that the brick was put there by a supernatural being to fix the wall. A tiny move would cause the collapse of the wall. Therefore the brick was kept there and never moved. It can still be found there today on the tower of the Jiayuguan Pass.

The Legend of Meng Jiangnu

Meng Jiangnu's story is the most famous and widely spread of all the legends about the Great Wall. The story happened during the Qin Dynasty (221BC-206BC). It tells of how Meng Jiangnu's bitter weeping made a section of the Great Wall collapse. Meng Jiangnu's husband Fan Qiliang was caught by federal officials and sent to build the Great Wall. Meng Jiangnu heard nothing from him after his departure, so she set out to look for him.

231

Unfortunately, by the time she reached the great wall she discovered that her husband had already died. Hearing the bad news, she cried her heart out. Her howl caused the collapse of a part of the Great Wall. This legend has been spread widely through textbooks, folk songs and traditional operas. It is well-known in China.

Tricking the Marquess with beacon fires

There was a very cruel and corrupt King You in Western Zhou Dynasty (1046 BC - 771 BC). He had a very beautiful concubine named Bao Si, but she never smiled. To entertain her, the King took Bao Si to the beacon towers and ordered to light the alarming fire of the Beacon Towers. The marquesses and soldiers saw the fire, thinking that western tribes came to invade, and then hurried to assemble. To their disappointment, they were teased and there was no tribal invasion. They were extremely depressed and went back angrily. Seeing their reaction, Bao Si finally burst into laughter. Soon after, enemies really invaded. The King ordered to light the fire to call his army, but no one came to rescue him. As a result, the capital was captured by the enemy, the King was killed, and Western Zhou Dynasty perished.

Zhaojun going out on the frontier pass

This is a true Great Wall story in Chinese history. In 54BC, Huhanye Chanyu, a tribal leader of the Huns, was defeated by his brother and escaped south to the Guanglu, just outside the Great Wall. He surrendered to Han court, and asked to be the son-in-law of then Emperor Hanyuan. After, Wang Zhaojun, a beautiful palace lady was selected and titled "princess" to marry Huhanye. After Zhaojun left her hometown, went through the Yumenguan Great Wall, departed the frontier and arrived in Huns area, she got along well with Huns and taught them the culture of the central plains. Since then, Huns and Han people had lived in peace for 60 years without a war. Zhaojun's contribution brought peace, tranquillity and prosperity to the Hus as well as the Han people.

Badaling Great Wall Legend - Poisonous Grass Helps Guard Against Enemies

It is said that after the construction of Badaling Great Wall, there were soldiers guarding there. When night fell, the sentinels were afraid that they would fall asleep and let the enemy come up without knowing it, so they pleaded God not to let them fall asleep. When the Jade Emperor knew it, he sent God of Medicine to sprinkle the seeds of a kind of poisonous grass outside the Great Wall. The grass grew up and it was all over the place. If the invading enemy came across the grass, they would be stung and shouted out, so that the sentry knew the enemy was coming. Ever since, th soldiers on guard had not been afraid of falling asleep at night anymore.

Jinshanling Great Wall Legend – Slates of Wangjing Tower

On the Tiger Mountain of the Jinshanling Great Wall, there is a Wangjing Tower surrounded by dangerous cliffs on all sides. It is said that many people were injured or even died transporting the slates to build the tower. Even though the slates could not be transported to the mountain top successfully. Hearing that, the God Jade Emperor was moved and sent God Erlang to help them. The God Erlang turned his sword into a whip and waved it to the slates. The slates immediately turned into many goats and went straight to the mountain top one by one. After the God Erlang reached the top, he counted, no more and no less, the slates were just enough to build the tower. At this time, a soldier screamed and ran back when seeing the God Erlang and the goats. The God was also shocked and kicked dozens of slates down to the mountain by accident. Therefore, dozens of slates to build Wangjing Tower were missing. Now, if you board Wangjing Tower, you can see that five of the twelve-layer foundation of the Wangjing Tower are made of gravel blocks and some slates are still piled up in the bottom the valley.

The wall stabilizing brick in Jiayguan Great Wall

According to this Great Wall legend, in the Ming Dynasty (1368-1644), there was a craftsman named Yi Kaizhan who was proficient in mathematics. He calculated that 99,999 bricks were needed to build Jiayuguan Pass. The supervisor did not believe him and said that if he mistakenly estimated it, all the workers would be sentenced to three years of hard labour as punishment.

After the project was completed, a brick was left behind. The supervisor was very happy and was prepared to punish the workers. However, Yi said that the entire city would collapse if the brick was moved. Since then, the brick was remained in place to stabilize the whole pass, and no one dared to move it. You can still find the brick on the Jiayuguan Pass today.

Legend of Yanmenguan Pass – Generals of the Yang Family

From the Warring States Period (475 - 221 BC) to the Ming Dynasty (1368 - 1644 AD), Yanmenguan Pass had been an important defense fortress on the border. The story of generals of the Yang Family occurred in the early years of the Song Dynasty (420 - 479), mainly talking about Yang's famous generals Yang Ye, Yang Yanzhao and Yang Zongbao and other Yang family members who defended the country against invaders. Yang Ye was a general of the Song Dynasty and led his seven sons to guard Yanmenguan Pass. He was loyal to the Song Dynasty, but he was finally killed by the traitor. His son and grandson have inherited and carried forward the good family style of Yang's "loyalty to the country and people".

Wu Sangui opened Shanhaiguan pass to surrender to the Qing Army

This is also a Great Wall story truly happened. In the late Ming Dynasty (1368-1644), the Ming court was threatened by the peasant uprising led by Li Zicheng and the Manchu army from northeast. When the Ming emperor committed suicide, which meant the demise of the Ming Dynasty, Wu Sangui and his army were at Shanhaiguan Pass of Great Wall. Knowing the importance of Wu Sangui and Shanhaiguan, Li kidnapped Wu's family to force him to surrender. In order to save his family, Wu prentended to surrender to Li, while asked Dorgon, the general of Manchu army for help in condition of giving Manchu some territories within Shanhaiguan. Li didn't relize Wu's trick until he arrived at Shanhaiguan when Li and his army had lost the favorable opportunity to enter Shanhaiguan Pass. At that time,

Dorgon came with his troop, defeated Li and forced Wu to surrender. Having no way out, Wu handed over Shanhaiguan Pass to Dorgon, and then Dorgon with Qing army entered central plain, occupied Beijing and established the Qing Dynasty (1644 – 1911).

Long-time preserving lime and Yanjing Town

During the Spring and Autumn Period and the Warring States Period (770 - 221 BC), King of Yan State requisitioned the farmers to build a high wall on the mountain top of his state's border to avoid the invasion by enemies. At that time, the walls were built with mud. By chance, the farmers discovered the lime which could make the wall more solid and began to build walls with it. Later, when Emperor Qin Shi Huang built the Great Wall, he specifically asked the people of the original Yan State to make lime, because the quality of the lime they made was very good and can be preserved for thousands of years without deterioration. Later, in order to reward Yan people, Emperor Qin ordered to construct a town for them. The town was named Yanjing, nowadays' Beijing.

CHINESE POEMS

咏鹅 - YǑNG É – AN ODE TO THE GOOSE by 骆宾王 / Luò bīn wáng

鹅、鹅、鹅，Goose, goose, goose,

(é é é)

曲项向天歌。You bend your neck towards the sky and sing.

(qū xiàng xiàng tiān gē)

白毛浮绿水，

(bái máo fú lǜ shuǐ) Your white feathers float on the emerald water,

红掌拨清波 Your red feet push the clear waves.

(hóng zhǎng bō qīng bō)

悯农 - MǏN NÓNG – TOILING FARMERS by 李绅 / Lǐ shēn

锄禾日当午，Farmers weeding at noon,

(Chú hé rì dāng wǔ,)

汗滴禾下土。Sweat down the field soon.

(hàn dī hé xià tǔ.)

谁知盘中餐，Who knows food on a tray

(Shuí zhī pán zhōng cān,)

粒粒皆辛苦。Thanks to their toiling day?

(lì lì jiē xīn kǔ)

七步诗 QĪBÙSHĪ – SEVEN STEPS VERSE by 曹植 / Cáozhí

煮豆燃豆萁，Lighting the bean stalk to boil the beans,
(Zhǔ dòu rán dòu qí,)
豆在釜中泣。and of this the beans thus wailed:
(dòu zài fǔ zhōng qì.)
本自同根生，"Borne are we of the same root;
(Běn zì tóng gēn shēng,)
相煎何太急 should you now burn me with such disregard?"
(xiāng jiān hé tài jí)

"春晓 CHŪNXIǍO – SPRING MORNING by 孟浩然 Mèng hào rán

春眠不觉晓，I wake up with the sun up high.
(Chūn mián bù jué xiǎo,)
处处闻啼鸟。Birds chirp everywhere in the sky.
(chù chù wén tí niǎo.)
夜来风雨声，Last night a rainstorm passed by.
(Yè lái fēng yǔ shēng,)
花落知多少 Flowers must have fallen down.
(huā luò zhī duō shǎo)

静夜思 JÌNG YÈ SĪ - THOUGHTS IN THE SILENT NIGHT by 李白 / Lǐbái

床前明月光， Moonlight reflects off the front of my bed.

(Chuáng qián míng yuè guāng,)

疑是地上霜。 Could it actually be the frost on the ground?

(yí shì dì shàng shuāng.)

举头望明月， I look up to view the bright moon,

(Jǔ tóu wàng míng yuè,)

低头思故乡。 And look down to reminisce about my hometown.

(dī tóu sī gù xiāng.)

ARCHITECTURAL DEVELOPMENTS

PAGODA - *Tǎ*

The Pagoda is essentially a tower, except more decorative and diverse in design. The Pagoda has spread across Asia and they have taken on many different roles in the many societies they overlook. Most commonly these highly decorated structures are Buddhist or Taoist and overlook a feature, thus acting like a watch tower or mark.

The structure itself is also unique in the fact that the interior is tailored to the Pagoda's purpose. Some are hollow, some are fortified. More often than not they will have an alter to pray at and a staircase, allowing the visitors to rise to the top. Pagoda's 'floor' plan are always set to an odd number.

BRIDGES

By 2019 there were 878,300 road bridges in China. What was once a pinnacle feature to many a myth and legend is now just another industrial aspect to the national infrastructure. Bridges have evolved from functional features showcasing architectural and artistic excellence to characterless, albeit impressive mega-constructions. How they evolve, and whether they will return to a form of showcasing beauty and character is something we shall see in the coming years.

TULUO

Tuluo roughly translates to earthen building. The reality of this traditional communal residence is far greater. These circular structures house the families and communities of the Hakka people, located in Fujian, South China. The main building structure surrounds a protected court yard or shrine. Historically the Tuluo were occupied by clan groups, The oldest still in existence, called Yuchanglou dates back to 1308 and the time of the Yuan Dynasty.

THE GREAT WALL

The Great Wall of China is not just an architectural development. It holds many of the stories and fabric of the modern nation today. Whilst the Ming dynasties development of the wall is the most famous, dated at 1368–1644 it has in fact been subject to change by near enough every historical dynasty. So much so that between the reconstructions and conflicts there are gaps in known history. There are quite literally mysteries and fortunes still to be found in and around the Wall and it's purpose as a defence system has soon transitioned into arguably the most interesting piece of architecture on the planet.

SHANGHAI IN 1990

SHANGHAI IN 2010

NANJING VERTICAL FORESTS

''The Nanjing Vertical Forest intervention is the first of its kind created by
Stefano Boeri Architetti in Asia and is located in the Nanjing Pukou District,
an area selected to lead the Southern Jiangsu modernization process and the
development of the Yangtze River area.'' - FROM Stefano Boeri Architetti
Website.

As China's pollution continues to rise in the megacities, so too will the
infrastructure projects needed to restore balance. The vertical forests are the
first of many new systems reshaping the face of China.

THE TEN GREAT BUILDINGS

There are ten public buildings in China which were constructed to
commemorate the ten years of Communist rule. All of which were in Beijing
they have since turned into core tourist attractions and functional buildings
that run the nation.

The Ten Great Buildings were managed under the urban initiative of the
Great Leap Forward, which propelled China from instability into a nation
state under Chairman Mao. The velocity of this development has continued
to this day.

The Ten Great Buildings are; The Great Hall of the People / The National
Museum of China / The Cultural Palace of Nationalitie / The Beijing railway
station / The Workers Stadium / The National Agriculture Exhibition Hall /
The Diaoyutai State Guesthouse / The Minzu Hotel / The Overseas Chinese
Hotel / The Chinese People's Revolutionary Military Museum.

244

GREAT HALL OF THE PEOPLE

NATIONAL MUSEUM OF CHINA

BEIJING RAILWAY STATION

MILITARY MUSEUM OF THE CHINESE PEOPLE'S REVOLUTION

THE
MINZU
HOTEL

NATIONAL AGRICULTURE EXHIBITION HALL

THE CULTURAL PALACE OF NATIONALITIES

THE DIAOYUTAI STATE GUESTHOUSE

WORKERS STADIUM

246

CHINESE QUOTES

- ✗ Dig the Well Before You Are Thirsty

- ✗ Teach a Man to Fish

- ✗ One Only Learns From One's Mistakes

- ✗ It's Better to Make Slow Progress Than No Progress at All

- ✗ Opportunity Knocks But Once

- ✗ Learn to Walk Before You Run

- ✗ The Master Leads You to the Door, the Rest is Up to You

- ✗ He who asks a question is a fool for five minutes; he who does not ask a question remains a fool forever

- ✗ Blessings come in disguise

- ✗ It's better to walk thousands of miles than to read thousands of books.

- ✗ Too many cooks spoil the broth.

- ✗ Happiness is the best cosmetic.

- ✗ Ignorance is bliss.

- ✗ Fate brings people together from far apart

- ✗ A gentleman's friendship is insipid as water

- ✗ hen entering a locality follow the local customs

- ✗ In hardship we see true friendship

- ✗ Men of different principles don't work well together

- ✗ Love isn't about having, it's about enjoying

- ✗ In a lover's eye is the foremost Beauty

- ✗ The harvest moon is brightest; every festival homesickness multiplies
- ✗ Even an upright official finds it hard to settle a family quarrel.
- ✗ Family shames must not be spread abroad
- ✗ If you don't run the family, you don't know the value of fuel and rice
- ✗ It takes more than one cold day for a river to freeze a meter deep
- ✗ All things are difficult at the start
- ✗ Failure is the mother of success.
- ✗ A day's planning is done at dawn
- ✗ Enduring deepening pain is how man ascends
- ✗ A book is a pocket garden
- ✗ Facts beat eloquence
- ✗ As distance tests a horse's strength, time reveals a person's character
- ✗ Repay good with good
- ✗ A person leaves a reputation, as a swallow leaves its call
- ✗ When adversity comes, receive it favorably
- ✗ Replace weapons with jade and silk

结束

THANK YOU FOR READING

IF YOU HAVE ANY QUESTIONS, IDEAS OR FEEDBACK DON'T HESITATE TO CONTACT ME OR LEAVE A REVIEW.

NOTES + IDEAS

Printed in Great Britain
by Amazon